Praise for Rich Hamilton's breakthrough book, *Disney Magic: Business Strategy You Can Use at Work and at Home*...

"Your book is a veritable Disney BIBLE! You've told the well-known stories, but added the creative thinking, smart planning, and constant "change" to make it all work. Walt was a dear, dear friend of mine and our families were close."

—**Art Linkletter, radio-television personality and author,**
Old Age is Not for Sissies and *Kids Say the Darndest Things*

"Loaded with information and easy to read! Rich Hamilton has combined stories about Walt Disney with useful success methods that Disney used to create Disneyland. If you like Disneyland, or have ever wondered how Walt Disney came up with the idea and successfully put the business together, read this book."

—**Jim Cathcart, author,**
The Eight Competencies of Relationship Selling

"Rich Hamilton dissects the magic of Disney in a fun, interesting and user-friendly way. "Disney Magic" clearly is a book of business savvy you can adapt to use personally and professionally."

—**Larry James, CelebrateLove.com, author,**
How to Really Love the One You're With

"Rich Hamilton captures the essential quality of Disney's genius. You're given a rare opportunity of stepping inside the mind of a visionary by exploring the dimensions of Walt Disney's dreams. This book is a "must read" for anyone seriously striving to obtain personal or professional success."

— **Carole Copeland Thomas, radio personality, author,**
Personal Empowerment

"Rich Hamilton helps with more than selling and marketing, he knows how to deliver on a dream, plan complex projects, and put together a responsive workforce. Listen carefully to what Rich says about engineering a successful business."

—**Bill Brooks, author,** *High Impact Selling*

"Rich Hamilton insists that we can all succeed by applying a few simple methods. Rich's down-to-earth way of looking at business is refreshing. Hamilton is at his best when discussing such specifics as how to give people what they want, how to understand promotion, and how to generate follow-up business."

—**James Malinchak, author,** *From College to the Real World*

Books by Rich Hamilton:

*Disney Magic: Business Strategy
You Can Use at Work and at Home*

*Internet Business Magic: Using Disney's
Magic Strategy in Your Own Online Business*

*Disney Magic Ideabook: Using Disney's Magic
Strategy for Your Own Business Success*

Internet Support:

www.MagicStrategy.com

Technical Resource Links:

www.InternetBusinessMagic.com

Internet Business Magic
Using Disney's Magic Strategy
In Your Own Online Business

*"Disneyland will always be
building and growing and adding new
things... new ways of having fun, of
learning things and sharing the
many exciting adventures
which may be experienced here."*
—*Walt Disney*

Rich Hamilton

SellBetter Tools
Phoenix, Arizona, USA

Internet Business Magic

First Edition
Copyright © 2004 Rich Hamilton. All Rights Reserved.

ISBN 0-9728476-1-8
Library of Congress Control Number: 2003097370

Publisher's Cataloging-in-Publication Data
(Prepared By Cassidy Cataloguing Services, Inc.)

Hamilton, Rich.
    Internet business magic : using Disney's magic strategy in your own online
business / Rich Hamilton. — 1st ed. — Phoenix, Ariz. : SellBetter Tools,
2004.
        p. ; cm.
    Includes bibliographical references and index.
    ISBN 0-9728476-1-8
        1. Electronic commerce. 2. Internet marketing. 3. Management.
    4. Business planning. 5. Success in business. 6. Walt Disney Company.
    I. Title.
HF5548.32 .H36 2004   2003097370
658.8/72—dc22   CIP

Schools and Corporations: This book is available at quantity discounts with bulk purchases for educational or business use. For more information please contact the publisher at the address below.

SellBetter Tools
Box 50186, Phoenix, AZ 85076 • 1-888-240-4742

Manufactured in the United States of America

Acknowledgments

There are so many people I can thank for their help and encouragement as I was writing this book. To Beverly Belury, who was thrilled with my book, *Disney Magic: Business Strategy You Can Use at Work and at Home,* but wanted me to talk to her group about building an effective internet website. She told me, "You could do both, you know, talk about the internet but frame it with the Disney business model."

To Pete Charlton, who, in 1978, showed me how to make a desktop computer run a business, and led me to begin programming. And to David Rayl, who, in 1987, counseled me on how to build a consulting business.

To Len White and Len Dozois, who gave me the tools and the market I needed to develop an international software business. To Richard Davis, Mike Britten, Michael Jacquot, Dennis Sykes, Mike Vivien, and the others on my beta test team who patiently questioned my instructions and crashed the software so it would stand up to everyone's use. And to the thousands, perhaps millions, of computer users around the world who never knew my name but who have used my software.

To Rick Hubbard, who, in 1990, taught me how to use email effectively, years before America Online or the world wide web.

To Sergey Brin, Cory Rudl, Danny Sullivan, Simon Grabowski, Ken Evoy and Tom Antion, who helped me understand the working of a "real" search engine strategy.

To Ken Pollock, Richard Davis, and David Rayl who offered me invaluable technical assistance as I fine-tuned the manuscript.

To Bill, Ted, and Nancy, whose problems highlighted what was needed. And to Nancy, Gwen, and Tony, who made it clear that they needed a "step at a time" approach.

To my wife and editor, Sharon, who has little interest in computers but became excited about the internet as she read the manuscript for this book.

And of course, to Walt Disney, whose inspiration and example proves that so much can happen if we only have the courage to make our dreams come true.

*"I believe in being
an innovator."*
–Walt Disney

Contents

Preface

This is not your typical computer book, loaded with buzzwords and technical diagrams. I've read plenty of those books. Perhaps you have, too.

This is not a typical business book, either. I'm tired of books that give lofty visions without specific how-to technology.

As you read this book, you will discover the methods and resources you need to effectively put your business online.

In creating this book, I've tried to merge the exciting business strategy of Walt Disney's theme parks with the emerging online business opportunity.

The result is a "business kit" that provides concepts, ideas, detailed instruction, and substantial additional resources to help plan, design, and execute an online business strategy.

To put it all together you'll want three things:

1. This book.

2. Online access to our special website.

3. The book, *Disney Magic–Business Strategy You Can Use at Work and at Home,* for additional insight into the Disney business.

I've been doing business online since 1983 and developing websites for my own company since 1997. I've done things that work, and tried things that don't work. There are lots of things in that latter category, and I've learned from each one.

I've also done most of it the hard way.

Over the years I tried to give my friends the information they needed to create their own online business. I found it was far too complex. There had to be an easier way, one that combined ease with a good business model.

Eventually, the art of the internet evolved to the point that it could be easier, and the business model evolved as well.

This book is the "front end" to the answer.

You see, I want you to do it the easy way! And I want it to work for you. (I *think* you want that, too. *Right?)*

How this book works

This skinny book is really over 800 pages long. That's because it's the "front end" to a website that is loaded with pages and pages of resources you'll want to use to put together your own website.

If 800 pages seems like a lot, be reassured that at our special website you'll only have to read, download, and use the things that are right for you.

And because it's in a website, it can change and be kept up to date. That makes this book very dynamic and powerful.

In some ways everything is new and different. And in other ways, it's all the same; nothing changes.

Which is why we can apply Walt Disney's business strategy to an online business.

The online information will change from time to time as we find new and better resources for you. Check back often. And be aware that because of this, the resources you find may be somewhat different than those we describe here.

Here's the website:

InternetBusinessMagic.com

You've heard of it somewhere? Of course! It's the name of this book.

The book and the website are closely linked. At various points throughout this book, particularly for technical information, you'll find an icon like this:

Check Resources
www.InternetBusinessMagic.com

This icon is a reminder to go online to find more information on the topic, to find the latest online courses, downloadable ebooks, and suppliers of services to help you easily build a profitable online business.

Disney as innovator

I've studied Walt Disney extensively, and I'm confident that he would have embraced the use of computers in his business, and he would have embraced the internet.

Because Walt was an innovator. He was the first to add sound to animated cartoons, the first to create a color cartoon, the first to create a feature length animated movie. Disneyland was another innovation, as were his ideas for EPCOT in Florida.

Not long ago, I was asked, "Why does it have to be so hard and so expensive to get a good, profitable website running?"

The honest answer? It should be easy and not too expensive!

But there are plenty of people out there who are willing to take your money (lots of your money) to do the job for you.

Maybe you've experienced them.

Several times a year I get an invitation with two free tickets to a special seminar about the internet. I've never gone, but I've known people who went, got excited, and invested several thousand dollars to establish an internet business.

But they're still at their old jobs. And they say the "internet deal" was a waste of time and money.

The beauty of the internet is that you don't have to invest a lot of money to establish an online business. (And you don't have to buy ads on the Super Bowl to promote it, either.)

The beauty of this little "business kit" is that you can buy it for so little. It should cost five hundred or a thousand dollars, maybe more.

I could base a consulting business around this material and charge ten to fifty thousand dollars per client to get things started.

But by packing it into a skinny little book, and backing it up with an internet website, I keep your costs down. Sure, you have to do a *little* of the work, but you'll save a lot and learn a lot, and that will translate to your bottom line.

—Rich Hamilton

Section 1: Foundation

You compete with Disney

When I was researching the Disney theme parks I came to a startling fact:

You are in competition with The Walt Disney Company and every other company that provides amazing customer service.

I don't care what you sell or where you are. Your customers, and your employees, have been to Disneyland or Walt Disney World. Or they have friends who have been there. They have experienced the very best customer service. They compare *you* with *that*.

How do you measure up?

What does this have to do with an online business? Everything.

Because it's true in a conventional, offline business. And it's true online, too. Online, it may be even more important, because online, customers can go *anywhere*. And it's *easy* for them to forget about you.

You compete with Disney.

Get ready now, and do it well.

You're in the Entertainment Business

Walt Disney knew he was in the *entertainment business,* and he knew that when he developed Disneyland (and Walt Disney World) it was an extension of that business.

You're in the entertainment business, too. You just didn't know it until today.

Maybe you're a dentist, a teacher, a computer scientist, or a grocer. Maybe you repair automobiles or do landscaping. It doesn't matter.

Your success depends on your ability to delight your customers.

Walt wanted his *guests* to leave Disneyland with *smiles* on their faces. And *you* have the same challenge.

You want your customers to conduct their transaction with a smile. You want them to smile when they're done. You want them to smile when they think of you and recommend you to others. You want them to smile when they come back for more.

What does Disney have to do with *your* online business?

The successful Disney theme park business model gives us many sound business principles that apply to *any* business.

The internet business experience has proven profitable to those firms who have implemented these sound business ideas as part of the online enterprise. (Sadly, in the early years online, few companies chose the sound business method, thinking that the internet itself was going to be a gold mine.)

So the point is this: I want you to run your online business as a sound business, whether it's a stand-alone online business or part of a large or small thriving firm.

Before we get too far into this, I want you to be aware that there are lots of ways to spend money trying to develop a business.

Bill's Bank Account was Attacked!

One of my friends, Bill, was grumbling about his internet website. (I won't reveal Bill's full name, but he's a nationally known professional speaker. It wouldn't surprise me if you have heard him speak.)

Bill invested about $30,000 to have a beautiful website to sell his products and services. It was beautiful, but it didn't work very well. And Bill was out 30 grand.

So Bill hired another designer. Another 30 grand. This one was really fancy. Flash openings, streaming audio and video. Wow! It looked great. Still, it didn't sell anything.

Last time I heard Bill talk about his website, he was looking for another designer. It seems his site didn't earn much, and his designer took weeks to make changes that needed to be done right away.

Bill doesn't want to deal with it, so he throws money at the problem. When he finally decides to deal with it himself, he'll find there are special tools to make it easy.

You'll find those tools right here.

Ted's Great Frustration

Not too long ago I sent an email to Ted, another professional speaker. The email was returned to me, undeliverable, so I called Ted to tell him his mailbox was full. His response was frustration. He said his email didn't work and his whole website was a disaster. All it was showing was an "Under Construction" page. The people who were supposed to make it work were not getting it done. And he asked if I would help him fix it.

You might call me a techie, when it comes to computers and the internet. I'm enough of a nerd that I understand this stuff. Most people don't, and if they do, they don't have the time to deal with it all. So, like Ted, they ask me to help.

Ted would like to do it himself, but it's too complicated. At least, it's been too complicated until now.

Ted is about to discover that he can tackle his website all by himself, and have it look good, draw traffic, and develop business.

Because Ted is going to use the information you're reading right here.

Nancy's been waiting a whole year!

Not long ago I heard from my friend Nancy. She's an author and publisher, and needs a website to promote her books.

She has contracted with a leading vendor in her field for a website, but has been waiting over a year and still has nothing. She's desperate. She called and said, "Rich, they're not getting anywhere. *I've paid them a bunch of money*, but now I'm calling you because I just need to get something going."

You see, she talked to a mutual friend who worked with me and had a small website up in 48 hours. Nancy has been waiting a whole year!

To be fair, it's partly her fault for not getting them the information they need. She needs to do it herself the easy way.

The answers are right here in this book.

What is the internet?

First, let's deal with what the internet is *not*. The internet is not a magic replacement for good business sense.

The dot-com crash of 2000-2002 proved that. In the five years leading up to that crash, the internet grew rapidly, but business speculators invested lavishly and unwisely in business models that suggested the internet would take over commerce.

While dot-com companies were going broke, and stocks were diving, some companies succeeded. A very few created a unique internet business that survived and thrived. Most of the successes came from companies who used the internet as an additional channel or tool to parallel or support their existing successful business.

Even Disney unwisely jumped in and acquired go.com, with unrealistic expectations. Ultimately, they shut down most of the go.com operation, and turned it into a central Disney *service and support site*. As I write this, at go.com you'll see information and links to the various Disney divisions and activities. It's evolved into a remarkable resource.

So what is the internet? It's another channel for doing business. It's a tool to enhance your business. It's...

A computer network. You use computers to automate your business so certain things are done quickly, accurately, and cheaply.

When you can automate business functions on the internet, linking your computers with many others, you save money and improve customer service.

A communications network. Email is the front line in using the internet as a communications tool. Other reporting systems and interactivity tools expand communications between employees and with customers. Online training and customer surveys automate certain aspects of the communications process. Some companies are even switching *telephone* service to the internet.

An information network. Your website can contain information useful to customers, prospective customers, and employees. Search engines make it possible to locate information you would not find otherwise. Links between sites lead you to even more information.

A transaction network. The network is capable of handling financial transactions with reasonable security and even delivering some products and services (information products, airline tickets, movie tickets, etc.)

Even in a small business, you want to utilize each of these networks to some extent.

Watch out!

The internet world is full of traps. It's much like getting your car repaired (only worse). Many of the rip-offs come from vendors who think they re providing true value.

There are several kinds of outfits out there:

1. Scam artists. They're out to grab your money, take over your resources, and take whatever they can.

2. Suckers. These folks were taken in by scam artists, "invested" in some kind of internet business, and now they're out "helping" others lose *their* money. You can feel bad for these folks; they're victims. But don't give them any money.

3. Well-intentioned "techies." These are designers, hosting companies, and information providers that want to help you. They look good and sound good, but they haven't got a clue about really marketing a business profitably, on the internet or anywhere else. Some of them actually provide a decent service. But that doesn't mean it's going to be profitable for you.

4. Legitimate, reasonably priced service providers who really do provide true value.

Sometimes, it's hard to know the difference. Here are the kind of stories I hear all the time:

"My web designer charges only $40 an hour. That's a good rate, isn't it?"

There is no such thing as a good rate. What matters is the bottom line. How much did you earn, and what did it cost?

Most designers will not focus on your needs. They tend to focus on high tech programming, beautiful design, or both. They talk marketing, but have little understanding of real online marketing.

Recently I heard the self-proclaimed "leading website developer" in the publishing business brag that his company developed websites that sell. I've seen some of those websites. They were hard to navigate and it was hard to locate products. They were low on technology, and low on design. The only reason his company is a leader is because they sell their services well. Not because they sell their customers' products.

Walmart and Amazon.com can afford to invest and waste a lot with website designers and programmers. You can't. Don't.

"I got an email offer to buy thousands (or millions) of email addresses that I can use to try to email my offer."

That's called spam. In some states, it's illegal. In every state it's unwelcome. I get hundreds of unwanted emails every week.

Send out spam, and your internet providers will probably cut off your service. Don't do it.

Sometimes they tell you that these are opt-in lists, meaning that the people on the list have requested being on the list. That means nothing to you. Those people still do not know you. They didn't ask *you* to be on your list.

Sometimes they say they will mail it for you. As I was writing this, I received an (unwanted) offer to mail *one million* names for $169, or *10 million names* for $869. This is just as bad. If they do mail for you rather than just stealing your money, your Internet Service Provider (ISP) will still disconnect you as the complaints come rolling in about your email campaign.

Email marketing is valuable. But don't ever buy someone else's list. Build your own. I'll share how in a moment.

"My web designer is putting together a 'Flash' website. I'm not sure what it is, but others he's shown me look really neat."

Quick! Call him and cancel everything. You have a designer who loves the craft and knows nothing about marketing your products or services.

Flash is cool, but it slows down computers, doesn't work on some computers, and most people click past it because it's an annoyance.

"My sister's neighbor works for a dot-com company and she has offered to design my website."

Aren't you lucky. If she's any good, she's a specialist. Either she programs well, designs well, or neither. She has no idea what you really need, and she is used to working with a big budget and staff. That's not what you want.

"I found a college kid who will create a custom website for me."

Same story, only he's probably a techno-geek or an artist who will disappear when spring break comes along and be gone permanently when he graduates or drops out.

"I signed up for a service that will optimize and submit my website to over 100 search engines."

This is another rip off. There are only a few search engines where you want to submit your website, and they don't like automated submissions. If the search engines figure out you've done this, you may be blacklisted and won't show up at all. Don't pay for this. Just go to Google, follow the instructions, and submit it yourself.

You could also wait for them to find you. It won't take as long as some would have you believe.

What matters most is having lots of good, well-organized content on your website, links from other sites to your website, and a good recommendation.

The search engine robots (called "spiders") are remarkable, and they are constantly being changed to index websites in a different way. The best thing you can do is follow the ideas in this book and at our website. (Search engines change all the time.)

Why I share these "scare stories" with you

I'd really like to just tell you the good stuff, what needs to be done and how to go about it. And I'm about to do just that.

It reminds me of another story, about a computer, not about the internet.

My aunt Julie called me one day and said she needed to buy a new computer, and she wanted my help locating a good buy. I agreed to look.

I watched the ads, and when a good value showed up in the flyer for a major office supply firm, I emailed her with the details.

Two weeks later, I received an email from her saying a friend had suggested another firm. I replied that I stood by my original recommendation.

Another well-meaning friend

A few weeks after that, she emailed me again, after yet another friend suggested a different brand of computer.

I replied something to this effect:

"Julie, you asked me for my recommendation. I gave you a good one but you kept talking to other people.

"If you really want a computer, the one I recommended is from a good manufacturer and a good retailer, and it's a good price. It will do everything you need to do. The retailer still has it on sale.

"If, in fact, you plan to buy a computer, buy the one I recommended and be done with it.

"If, on the other hand, you intend to visit with everyone you know, get more confused, and not buy anything, that's okay with me, but I don't want to hear anymore about it."

Two days later, she called me. She and my uncle had bought what I recommended, and she was excited with her purchase.

The next day, my uncle called to thank me. "Julie has been driving me nuts talking to everyone about what to buy. Your email did the trick, and I'm not listening to all her confusion any more. Thank you!"

Still going...

As I write this some three years later, Julie is still delighted with that computer. It was a bargain and had enough computing power to carry her some years into her future needs.

I know that along the way to your internet project, you're going to have friends try to help you by suggesting other things you can do. And it's true, there are a lot of different ways to put together an internet business.

What I'm offering you in this book is a sound business approach, combined with all the high-tech tools you need, and a way to get it done without spending a fortune. (Overspending on ineffective technology was another cause of the dot-com crash of 2000-2002.)

If you want to add more confusion to your life, keep looking for another way.

Otherwise, just follow this book.

A thought about the business

You probably already know what you want to sell online, and may have some pretty good ideas about how you want to sell it.

When I'm discussing online business strategies, my clients often want to jump right in and create a website.

Hold on!

The first step is making a business plan.

"Ouch! That hurts," you're thinking.

It doesn't have to hurt. Your business plan can be a couple of pages describing how you're going to do business, or it can be an elaborate affair.

Are you doubting me right now? Then let me ask a few questions.

Have you researched the search engine keywords that will make you the most money?

Do you have an email strategy? Do you have an autoresponder strategy? Have you created a plan for sequential autoresponders?

Have you examined why your online customers will buy from you?

What do you want to say on your main page? What do you want to say on the other pages? Why?

I apologize for dropping buzzwords in here; I've done it to demonstrate the fact that there are a number of things to consider before you jump in and do it wrong.

Take a few minutes to think about and write up the foundation of your business, a short business plan.

You can write up your basic plan in under an hour. Let's get started!

Disney's success can lead you to your own success

The business culture at Disney theme parks is amazing. Everything is done by design; the reasons are well thought out.

The principles at Disney are well defined and are portrayed consistently so that the business procedures are clear to all. No one has to guess what to do.

I'm briefly going to cover what they do to establish a firm business foundation at Disney. For a more complete explanation, see my book, *Disney Magic: Business Strategy You Can Use at Work and at Home.*

Shortly after introducing Mickey Mouse, Walt knew he needed to appeal to an audience across the entire country. Because Walt was reared in Missouri, he had a clear understanding of Midwestern values.

As Disneyland neared completion in 1955, Walt recognized that the name "Disney" had taken on a life of its own, representing good, wholesome fun. Disney movies were expected to reflect that wholesomeness, and Disneyland had to reflect it as well.

Walt also knew that he wanted certain things to happen in Disneyland, based on his negative experiences in most other amusement parks to that time.

Three values were considered most desirable:
1. Walt wanted Disneyland to give guests a good show.
2. Walt wanted Disneyland to be spotlessly clean.
3. Walt wanted Disneyland to be staffed by clean, friendly people.

Disney was able to accomplish that when he built Disneyland. Today, over 35 years after Walt's death, customer surveys show that the three things guests report as most impressive at Disneyland and Walt Disney World are: (1) the good show, (2) the place is clean, and (3) the people are friendly, the very values Walt regarded as so important.

Walt recognized that the company would be hiring a lot of new people who needed to be taught about what Walt called "the whole package," or "the Disney system."

So he created a training department that he called "Disney University." It provides orientation training to new employees and continuing leadership training to all employees.

Traditions. One of the most unique parts of the orientation training is called "Traditions." It starts with values like honesty, reliability, loyalty, and respect for people as individuals.

Belief in innovation and a common focus are important at Disney. From values come the history and philosophy that make Disney theme parks what they are.

The training also focuses on various unique aspects of the Disney business culture so that new employees will understand what behavior is expected and will understand why things work like they do.

This unique approach makes it possible for cast members to make decisions based on reasons, rather than rules.

And, as we'll discuss in a moment, it's important to an online business, too.

Here are a few of the things in the Disney culture that are taught in the orientation:

A special language. Disneyland is seen as a large outdoor show, where everyone has an important role.

Disney has no customers. They play *host* to *guests*. A crowd is an *audience*.

The employees are *cast members*. Cast members work *onstage* or *backstage*. Uniforms are *costumes*. Instead of rides, they have *attractions* or *adventures*.

Today they call Disneyland (or the parks at Walt Disney World) a *theme park,* but in the early days of Disneyland it was an *environmental park*, or, just *Disneyland*. There wasn't anything else like it. It was *not* an "amusement park."

A first name policy. Walt said, "Call me Walt. The only 'Mr.' we have around here is Mr. Toad." When Disneyland opened, the cast members were given numbered identification badges, but soon these were changed to name tags that displayed their first name, making first names easy.

The Disney Look. Disney knew costumes would play an important role in creating the image he wanted. Costumes had to be designed right, kept clean and in good repair.

Beyond costumes, the cast members needed to project that clean, wholesome look that we think of as Disney. Neat, well-groomed cast members enhance the image. Walt didn't want the fantasy of Disneyland ruined by the encroachment of modern society and contemporary fashion and grooming.

Hair must be neat and trimmed. Jewelry is limited. Visible tattoos and body piercings are restricted.

The "Disney Look" has changed occasionally through the years. For some time no facial hair was allowed, but now men may sport conservative moustaches if they wish.

All this is made clear before cast members are hired, so there's seldom any problem later.

Take the risk *and* pay the bills

There were two key parts of the early Disney organization that forged a powerful business together.

Segment One was driven by *ideas*. Walt Disney was the idea man, constantly driving the company forward with new, often wild ideas.

Segment Two was the money or numbers man, embodied in the person of Walt's older brother, Roy Disney.

Walt constantly had ideas for new projects, and Roy constantly vetoed them, citing a lack of money or concern that the idea wouldn't pay off.

We often hear about how Roy would always find a way eventually, but I think there was more happening in this dual dynamic.

The conflict challenged Walt to improve and develop the best ideas until he could convince Roy to find the financing. Over time, Walt would give up on certain ideas, and develop the better ones until they would gain Roy's support.

That dynamic created a powerful balance in the Disney organization, where new ideas were encouraged but not exploited until they were grown into sound business plans.

Without Walt, the company surely would have collapsed due to the lack of story ideas and the creation of bold, new projects.

Without Roy, the company would have quickly been bankrupt due to Walt's exuberance over new projects with little attention to the business dynamic.

Both brothers were aware of their roles, and performed a "checks and balances" function on one another.

The service theme

Once the culture is identified and defined, it is translated into the operation.

That starts with the *service theme*.

Walt Disney expressed it like this, "My business is making people, especially children, happy." While Walt may have kept children in mind, he also wanted to entertain adults; that was one of the goals in building the park.

As Disneyland opened, the training described it very simply, "We create happiness."

At Disney today, it's "We create happiness by providing quality entertainment for people of all ages, everywhere."

I think it's interesting that the business is defined in terms of the customers' or guests' emotions.

Walt didn't define the business in terms of films, or cartoons, or toys, or even an amusement park. He didn't string together a list of seemingly unrelated businesses. Walt wanted to create happiness.

You'll want to write a Service Theme for your online business that defines the business in terms of what you're selling and who you're selling it to.

Core purpose

You may refine or focus your service theme into a "core purpose." Lee Cockerell, Executive Vice President of Walt Disney World Operations, says the core purpose is to "give every guest the best vacation they've ever had."

This simplifies the theme somewhat. When a guest is seated in a restaurant, it's easy to understand that the chairs need to be properly padded, the plates and silverware need to be clean, and the table shouldn't wobble.

So the facilities staff understands what they are doing when they are fixing tables, or upholstering chairs. The dishwashers understand that a dirty fork or glass will ruin the experience. The kitchen staff knows that the food must be right and presented or arranged beautifully.

The servers know that they must be attentive and not intrusive, because they play a role in giving the guests "the best vacation they've ever had."

Service standards

Disney's service standards are established to set standards for the work done while delivering on the Service Theme.

In the Disney theme parks, the service standards are: Safety, Courtesy, Show, and Efficiency.

Within each of these four areas, Disney establishes definitions and standards for the park and for each attraction.

Delivery systems

Delivery systems are established for:

Cast. The employees who create and deliver the products or services. Hiring, training, rehearsing, and taking care of the employees is covered in more detail in *Disney Magic*.

Setting. The setting is defined as "onstage," anywhere there is customer contact. It might include work or production areas that do not involve customer contact, if it's part of the deliverable.

Your website itself would be part of the setting, because it is a point of customer contact. The behind the scenes systems that process orders, which may also be part of the website computing systems, would fall under the category of operating systems.

Operating systems. All the behind-the-scenes systems that keep the organization running are included here. Think of systems for scheduling, production, purchasing and receiving, billing, banking and utilities.

When it's all operating correctly, the systems work together smoothly and guests don't even realize what's happening.

What to do now

Even though you probably know what it is you want to sell, take time now to write out the foundation statements of your business.

Write out a comprehensive history, philosophy, and mission statement. This will provide you with the basis for developing your business.

Follow that with the elements of your culture that you wish to make part of your workplace, as Disney did in areas of terminology, communication, and appearance. Write out the service standards for your online business. Combined with your Service Theme, these will be the basis for decision-making and planning for the short- and long-term.

Section 2:
Internet Business Strategy

Put on a Good Show

Disney's key concepts for Disneyland were deliver a "good show," a clean environment, and clean-cut, friendly employees.

Walt's background was in the movie business, and he was a great storyteller. He knew that amusement parks should be more entertaining, and he wanted his guests to leave with a smile on their faces.

It's a good concept for an internet website, too.

The power of a compelling story

The theme park concept, originated by Walt Disney at Disneyland, is poorly named.

Of course, Walt didn't call Disneyland a "theme" park. To Walt, is was just "Disneyland," or "Disneyland Park."

Because it was originally created with five "lands," and everything in a land or section of the park had to fit the "theme" of that land, eventually Disneyland and the competitors who followed were called "theme parks."

The real secret to the *charm and magic* at a Disney theme park goes way beyond the theme. It's the *compelling story* that creates the magic in each attraction.

At Disney, they talk about the "Power of Story." Walt Disney understood that his animated features succeeded when they told a compelling story. When he began designing Disneyland, he called on animators and designers who understood how Disney worked, and they designed rides and attractions around stories that were "told" as the guest took part.

Using a story provides several powerful benefits in an organization:

1. Stories create an emotional connection
2. They keep the culture alive
3. They communicate a vision
4. Stories convey the values of the organization and the leader

This same principle applies to other businesses. It's the story of your business that will intrigue your guests and make their visit enjoyable.

Your online business, too, will create a much more compelling presence if you present your website with an underlying story. That story can tie your entire website together (the "theme" of a land), and each page or attraction on the website can contain its own story within that overall theme.

"Clean"

Disney learned in the early years with Mickey Mouse that to have true success he needed to appeal to the largest available market. While his competitors sometimes would take their characters down somewhat unsavory paths, Walt charted out an entertaining but wholesome approach to animation. Walt's childhood was spent in Missouri, and he had a clear understanding of Midwestern values.

Planning Disneyland, Walt knew the place had to be spotless, as families would be comparing Disneyland to amusement parks littered with trash. "Clean" became a compulsion.

While you may be targeting a narrow market online, you still want to appeal to the largest possible audience. Like Walt in Disneyland, your best approach is to present a clean, easy to use website that appeals to broad, wholesome values.

Friendly

Amusement parks were often staffed by somewhat "scary" employees. Walt insisted that Disneyland's staff be clean-cut and friendly.

Online, you want to present a friendly website, with easy to use features. Communications should be happy and friendly.

Ordering, requesting newsletters, online courses, and locating information should be easy and fun. As your guests explore your website, they should find reasons to smile.

Deliver Magic Moments

In the *Disney Magic Business Strategy* book we examined how Disney strives to have every employee involved in creating "magic moments" for guests.

Sometimes these are personal, one-on-one interactions, and at other times they're "organized."

Magic moments fit three areas:

1. **High-touch Magic Moments.** Participating in the parade would be a prime example of this. A special one-on-one encounter between an employee and a guest would also be "high-touch." A high-touch Magic moment involves guest participation in an activity, beyond just being an observer or sitting on a ride.

Online you can do this, too, with quick, pleasant responses and interactions to orders and requests for information, telephone follow-up, bonus gifts, and free upgrades to shipping or delivery methods.

2. **High-show Magic Moments.** Disneyland parades could be considered high-show magic moments, as could many of Disney's attractions and locations. These involve vivid presentations, colorful, lush, grand appearance and sound. *Do this online by providing professional, colorful website pages to view and lots of useful information.*

3. **High-tech Magic Moments.** From making resort reservations, to checking in at the hotel and using the FastPass system, Disney has harnessed technology to build speed, accuracy, and expertise into service solutions. *Pursue all the possibilities with your website and automating as much of the delivery and service as possible.*

Make the decision to make delivering magic moments part of your offline *and online* business culture. Conduct business in a way that makes your customers smile.

Today, it's not enough to deliver what's expected. Deliver *more than what's expected, and deliver a nice surprise as well.*

Give them a pleasant surprise

One of the easiest ways to create a magic moment is to give your customer or prospective customer a pleasant surprise.

You will probably go to Disneyland to ride the rides.

And the first surprise you get is the beautiful landscaping. Just inside the entrance on a hillside is a giant image of Mickey Mouse, planted in beautiful, colorful flowers. At every turn you discover lush green trees and flower beds brimming with color.

Throughout Disneyland you hear beautiful music, piped in through a high quality stereo sound system. The music is selected to match the locale and the time of day.

Walking down Main Street you may encounter a barbershop quartet, performing 1900-era songs.

In the "hub" you may find the Disneyland Band.

And in New Orleans Square, look for a jazz combo.

These all delight the guests at Disneyland. Yet few, if any, went there for landscaping or musical treats.

What can *you* give *your guests* that will surprise them, treating them with *something unexpected?*

Susan is a friend of mine who sells real estate. Over the years, she has tried all the conventional "gifts" for her clients, including pens, magnets, and real estate shopping planners.

When she saw my *Disney Magic* book, she told me she had considered a number of different books about real estate for her clients, but most of them seemed too dry and didn't really convey the image she wanted to project.

But *Disney Magic* gave her an idea. Because it's a book that is written with success concepts for business managers, employees, and for people at home, she saw it as a gift that would be a complete surprise. When I told her she could buy them wholesale in case lots, she actually got excited.

What about online businesses?

Think about delivering surprises throughout the experience your *guest* has at your website.

Start with a pleasing design, with a simple, pleasant color scheme.

Over-deliver on your promise for information on the website.

Offer a free gift, in the form of a free online course or a series of useful articles, emailed every two or three days for ten issues or so, followed with a free newsletter subscription.

When someone makes a purchase, give them a free gift.

At my software business website, computer programmers who buy my specialized programming tools get a free copy of my SellBetter Estimator software, a program that assists them in preparing estimates and proposals for their clients. This isn't mentioned anywhere in the promotional material on the website... it's a surprise gift delivered with their purchase.

One author I know offered several complete books as ebooks to anyone who bought his new book online.

In the *Disney Magic* book, buyers are rewarded with membership in a special website devoted to additional information and reader experiences using the strategies in the book.

You can provide similar surprises for your visitors.

It's just another channel

Not long ago a good friend talked with me about moving his entire business to the internet.

"I want to quit sending 'snail mail,'" he said. "No more phones. Just do it all on the internet. That's where the business is going."

Big mistake.

It's just *another* channel.

A better idea would be "Follow the money."

Sure, if you can get your customers to do their order entry and reduce your overhead by going online, it's a good idea. But it's not the only idea.

In mid-2003, Cisco Systems (the people who make most of the internet routing equipment) reported that an astounding 90% of their business was handled online. Their customers enter their own orders online and, as a result, get faster, more accurate service.

What that statistic *doesn't* say is that even the people who had the most to do with inventing the internet still get 10% of their business the old-fashioned way, from customers who are buying *computer network* equipment!

If they said, "Nope, internet orders only!" they would lose 10% of their business. How smart would *that* be?

Southwest Airlines has been taking reservations and selling tickets (etickets!) at their own website longer than any other major airline. They sell more than 60% of their tickets that way.

So, 40% of their business still comes in the traditional ways, over the phone and at the ticket counter.

If they said "Our internet website only!" they would lose 40% of their business. Will they do that? Of course not.

Like many businesses, the 40% requires that they pay a telephone reservationist or airport ticket agent to take the information and enter it into their computer network. It's more costly, and the information still goes to the same place. Recognizing the cost differential, they often offer better fares on their internet website.

During the dot-com crash of 2000-2002, lots of firms went out of business or shut down their internet websites. Yet, during that same time period, internet buying increased. Lots of companies were doing it wrong.

One firm, Staples, the office supply company, realized that they had made a mistake. To attract investment money, Staples had created a separate corporation to run their online business. Soon they realized that it was just another channel, and that the online business shouldn't be separate. Giving investors of a profit on their investment, at great expense Staples bought back the online venture.

Even if your entire business is online, and you have no physical storefront, you will have customers who are uncomfortable ordering online. For them, be ready to fulfill orders received by phone, fax, and mail.

A friend of mine sends out 250,000 emails a month to his newsletter subscribers and takes orders for advertised products online, and by phone, fax, and mail every day... happily!

Let's remember Disney. You can buy theme park tickets online, at the Disney Store in the mall, at the Disney hotels, at nearby hotels, or at the main entrance.

It's just another channel.

Go for the business any way you can get it.

That means you take orders the conventional way *and on the internet*. It would be foolish to miss the channel. It would be equally foolish to ignore the other channels.

Your own domain

The first order of business when planning a website is that you need your own domain.

The domain is the name of your website, generally ending in ".com," ".org," ".net," ".biz," ".info," or any number of suffixes. (New ones are added regularly, and many countries have their own.)

Own your own

It's important that you own and control your own internet domain.

Even if an association or internet service provider makes space available, you want to send your customers and prospective customers to your own domain:

YourDomain.com

I've known companies who place their website with an association, and they end up with an address like:

mybiz.association.com or *association.com/mybiz.*

While it may be worthwhile to be listed and to post a profile with your associations or a marketing group, where available, that should not be your primary website, and should, in fact, refer people to your main website.

You do not want to promote *them,* you want to promote *you.*

I belong to an association who lists my name, photograph, and business profile on their website. They changed their name a couple of years ago, and they changed their website domain name. The old name disappeared. Any references to it in my old literature, business cards, emails, etc., would have instantly become unusable.

Of course, I had my own domain, so it wasn't a problem.

One of my clients very wisely snapped up a domain name back in 1995 that simply identified their industry, as in *industry.com.* I learned later they didn't own the name, they *used it* and their web developer owned the name.

After a few years, that web developer realized how valuable the domain was, and increased the annual price substantially.

My client couldn't afford it, and obtained a new domain name, adding their initials to the industry, as in *abcindustry.com.*

While the new name was okay, they had promoted the other address in advertising and brochures, and there was no way to correct all the ads that were already out in the marketplace. Even their email suddenly started going into an electronic trash bin somewhere. Don't let that happen to you.

What do you want in a domain name?

You want simple words, somewhat descriptive of what you do.

When we named this book, a considerable effort went into finding a name that could also be a website. *InternetBusinessMagic.com* was one of several hundred names we considered. We didn't title the book until we knew we could get the domain name.

There are some other factors to consider:

The .com Suffix

In the early days of the world wide web, the ".com" suffix was designated for commercial business, and because of its well-established use, it's the most desirable suffix for an online business.

Be sure your domain ends with .com.

Hyphens

Some domain names contain hyphens, which makes them easier to read but harder to say.

You could get a website like *how-to-sell.com* but it's hard to say out loud in a way that the listener knows how to enter it in their computer. You'd have to say, "How hyphen to hyphen sell 'dot-com.'"

I've even seen some where there are three words, and only one hyphen. That's a *really* confusing zinger.

Don't accept a domain name with hyphens.

Since a domain name can be entered in caps or lowercase without affecting how the website is found, words can be separated in print by capitalizing each word, as in:

InternetBusinessMagic.com

Confusing words

The how-to-sell example contains a confusing word, too, er... "to." It could be confused as *how-2-sell.com* or *how-too-sell.com* or *how-two-sell.com.*

Even my home website, *SellBetter.com,* is at a disadvantage because "Sell" can be confused with "Cell," a common error in this world of cell phones. As a result, I have to vocalize that well-established website very carefully, and I've started shifting business to:

MagicStrategy.com

Hard to spell words

Some words are hard to spell. For example, *CompellingStory.com* could be difficult because of difficulty spelling compelling. Is that one "l" or two?

Choose easily spelled words.

Similar characters

Certain letters and numbers can be confusing, too, if the meaning is not clear. Consider the following characters:

l, 1, and *I*

0 and *O*

You don't have to avoid those characters entirely, just be sure that what you use is what your customers would expect.

For example, it might look good to get:

lnternetbusinessmagic.com

but the first letter is a lowercase "L" and your customers won't get it right. This concept seems obvious but I've seen the domain names people have registered. It's appalling!

Funny spellings

Avoid funny spellings, too. *GR8* may be a great puzzle for your license plate but not for your domain.

Be sure your website is easy to read, spell, and speak!

Capitalize on misspellings

Misspellings can be a challenge, too. Don't use a misspelling unless it's part of the company name. Then, register both domains and set up the incorrect one to "redirect" guests automatically to the correct website.

As an example, The Vitamin Shoppe, a chain of retain health food stores that's active online, has their website set to accept three domains: *VitaminShoppe.com, TheVitaminShoppe.com,* and *VitaminShop.com.* All go to the same website.

Disney has lots of domain names, all designed to take you to various parts of the online Disney offering.

Looking for Disneyland? Go to *Disneyland.com.*

Want Walt Disney World? Go to *WaltDisneyWorld.com.*

Not sure where to go? Try *Disney.com.*

How do you set this up for your websites? Check our website for information.

Choosing a name

Now you know the domain success rules. How do you choose a name? Again, check our website for tools. Most obvious names are taken, so you'll have to search awhile. Be patient. As you work at it for awhile, you will discover some good names that are available.

Your website servers

Choose a *hosting company* who leases you space on their "server" computers to hold your web pages and online programs.

Some companies think they should run their own servers, but it's much easier to contract with someone who specializes in just that. You and your company will still control the content and what happens on your leased server.

But on Saturday night, when the server goes down, someone else has to fix it. And they'll usually fix it so fast you won't even know anything happened.

Compare that to having it in-house. On Saturday night, eventually you'll get the call that your website is not working. You'll have to find your computer techs, and get them to drive to the office to fix things. Within a few hours, they will get it done.

Do you think it's better because you have a fulltime IT staff taking care of things at your office? How long did it take them to fix things last time *your* computer broke?

Even giant internet portal companies like Yahoo! contract with private third-party providers for their data servers and internet connections. If it makes sense for them, it makes sense for you, too.

Check Resources
www.InternetBusinessMagic.com
Hosting company, Domain Names

Get your *own* email address

Listen closely. I've known a lot of people who have been burned for not following this advice.

You want your own email address, one that looks like: YourName@YourDomain.com

You are making a big mistake if you think you are okay with an address like *yourname@aol.com, you@msn.com,* or *you@earthlink.net.*

There are a bunch of reasons, many out of your control:

1. It promotes the ISP instead of YOU.
2. If the ISP changes you have to change anyway.
3. If you move you might have to change ISP.
4. Your ISP might go out of business.
5. Another ISP might offer a better "deal."
6. Another ISP might offer faster, more reliable service.
7. It looks amateurish. (At one time, an AOL address meant your were high tech. Now it's just like the kid down the street.)
8. You might want to change to cable service, or DSL, or wireless or satellite service.

Any and all of these things happen every day. And the sooner you fix it, the better.

Make Your Email Address Pay

One of the biggest challenges of business email is that when you establish your address at a local or national Internet Service Provider (ISP), you're stuck. You can't change without advising all your business contacts of your new address. And printing new business cards, stationery, and advertising.

Then you hope they all get it and don't forget. And you know the change is an inconvenience to your customers and prospects, and it looks bad.

I have many friends who have cable internet service, and once had addresses like *rich@home.com.* (I even had one, though I didn't use it.) When the @home internet service went bankrupt, they lost their email addresses.

Sure, they got new addresses, but again, all those business cards, emails, brochures, letters, and advertising that are already out there just lost the ability to connect. And when someone can't connect, they think you went out of business.

Your ISP could go out of business, merge, or discontinue your type of service, leaving you with this very problem.

Maybe your company has already covered this for you. If so, fine. But if your email address is not you@yourcompany.com, you have a problem. Addresses at aol.com, msn.com, mindspring.com, or home.com are just not professional anymore. And they're not portable. You need portability, so you can change providers.

Where do you get your own email address?

Your website hosting company will set up email addresses for you, using your own domain as part of the address.

Then, you can manage it two ways.

The first option is to have your email *forwarded* to the email address that's given to you by your local ISP. If you choose this option, and your email address is authorrich123@earthlink.com, all mail sent to your own email address will be instantly forwarded to your earthlink address. This is okay, because you still have control and if you change ISPs, all you have to do is tell your hosting company to start forwarding to your new mailbox.

The second option is to have your hosting company set up an actual mail account on your server, and you'll retrieve your mail from there.

Either way, be sure to set your email program so the "From" address is your own email address, not the ISP email address.

Check Resources
www.InternetBusinessMagic.com
Email address

What works on the internet today?

There are several ways for most businesses to make money on the internet today.

1. Sell your product (or service) directly from your internet website. Think in terms of an *online catalog*.
2. Use your website as a remote, interactive presentation machine.
3. Use your website to generate leads for more conventional selling.
4. Refer visitors at your website to the websites of other companies with whom you have developed a marketing relationship.
5. Employ existing auction websites to sell certain merchandise.

You'll probably want to *use all or most* of these methods.

Selling directly from your website

This is the "traditional" way of doing business on the web.

I remember the day Amazon.com ran their first full-page ad in *The Wall Street Journal*. They established this model on the internet in a big way, and lost millions of dollars doing it. Eventually, they started making a little money, but thousands of copycat businesses failed, fueling the dot-com crash of 2000-2002.

While I expect you will want your website to welcome guests who have seen your ads, read your brochures, or who just remember your website name, this will not be the big money maker for you.

It will, however, be a great source of repeat and referred customers.

And you've thought how wonderful it would be to put up a website and *sell everything you've got* in your online store.

In fact, this is what most people think of when they think of starting an online business. It's the traditional business model, moved over to the internet.

It's a wonderful idea, but it's not so simple. "Build it and they will come" makes a great movie, but seldom works out in business, especially online.

Because they have to find you first, and before they find you they have to *want* to find you.

Sell directly from your website? Yes! But it's a bit more complex than just putting up a store and expecting business as a result.

So plan on it. You'll want to make your products available on-line.

You could think of it like an online catalog. You can put your whole catalog online. Great idea?

Sure, but use the power of the internet to your benefit.

You've probably seen companies who put their catalog online, complete with a photograph of the item and a 50-word description.

That's how they did it with their printed catalog. But the reason they limited the information was because of the high cost of printing and mailing catalogs.

Online, everything is different. It's cheap to store more information, so offer pages of information on each item. Your guests will only open the pages of items they're interested in. You won't be printing it on paper or mailing it. So take advantage of this online opportunity.

I know a guy who has his computer set up to make the sound of a cash register every time an order comes in to his email system. And his computer sits in his office going "ka-ching!" 24 hours a day!

Yours can, too. Just plan on building your website right and promoting it, like you would any business.

Your remote, interactive presentation machine

I'm about to share with you a method of using your website to profitably build business that I've *never* heard any of the so-called internet gurus suggest. (Of course, once they read this book, that will change.)

Yet this method may be one you've already used, by accident.

When you design your website so that it contains all the materials, pictures, diagrams, and information that you might need when making a one-on-one sales presentation, you're ready to use this process.

It will work only with a customer or prospect who has internet access and can talk with you on the phone at the same time. (That means 80% of businesses and about half of the households in the US.)

It's this simple:

Instead of making a personal sales call, you make a phone call. If there's interest in seeing the presentation, you ask if they have internet access.

Give them your website and wait for them to report it's on-screen.

Now, begin the presentation, and tell them where and when to click on the screen. (You do the same thing at your computer, so you see what they see.)

You talk them through the sales presentation on the phone, responding as you would face-to-face, and showing them what you want them to see by leading them through your website.

This method is powerful.

In the early days of the internet, often websites were no more than an online brochure. They didn't do much, and have even less impact today.

But when you personalize the process by being "live" on the phone, leading them through the parts of your website that they need to see, *it's even more powerful* than a face-to-face presentation, because they are very actively involved.

Generate leads for conventional selling

Some services, big ticket items, and complicated products may not lend themselves to direct selling online, but the website can be used to develop a relationship, generate leads, and help maintain a relationship.

I'm almost afraid to suggest this, because as quickly as someone says it can't be sold online, their competitor comes along and beats them to the punch.

Once I talked with an insurance salesman who assured me long term care policies can only be sold face-to-face.

Three weeks later, I received a mail order offer from a different firm, complete with rates, order form, and health questionnaire. And it said I could call a toll-free number if I preferred, or go online.

The point is simple: The first guy I talked with had closed his mind to the possibilities (perhaps by his company's edict).

The second company was ready to do business however their customer wanted to do business.

Referring business to other websites

Amazon.com popularized the idea of affiliate programs back in 1997. Selling books, they realized that each of the special-interest websites on the internet could become a mini-bookstore, referring customers to Amazon and building the Amazon customer base substantially.

The affiliate (you) recommends books related to the subject of your website and provides links to the partner website (Amazon) using a special web address (called an "affiliate url").

The special url triggers software at the Amazon website so that if a purchase is made, Amazon pays the affiliate (you) a commission.

You don't have to write the book, stock it, pack it, ship it or collect for it.

As wonderful as this sounds, it only works if you have a lot of traffic coming to your website and responding to your "pre-sell" endorsement.

And that requires that you've built a relationship with your visitor.

Registration in a quality affiliate program costs nothing and *anyone* with enthusiasm and commitment can succeed. Representing high-value products or services as an affiliate is a great way to make some extra (sometimes substantial) cash. Surfers will always follow recommendations that put the customer's needs and wishes first so it's not difficult to earn commission income.

Auction merchandise

Use an existing auction website, like eBay, to sell certain merchandise, especially collectibles, discontinued merchandise, and hard-to-find products.

Lots of discontinued Disney merchandise is sold by Disney on eBay, often at about half price.

I bought a warm lined Disneyland jacket during one visit, when the weather was colder than I'd expected. The jacket was $75, a reasonable price for a good quality jacket.

The following winter, the identical jacket was on sale on eBay for half the price. It was brand new, being sold by Disney.

By that time at Disneyland they had a similar jacket, but with slightly different decoration. So the old jacket was discontinued merchandise.

Disney also sells art on eBay, discontinued prints, artwork removed from the Disney hotels, and promotional art originally developed for the theme parks.

They even sell their junk on eBay, figuring someone will see the old trade show booth as a valuable Disney artifact.

You could do some of that, too, at very low cost. Set up an auction program on eBay to sell your discontinued and returned merchandise. There's an international market out there on the internet, and for the most part, it won't affect your regular sales.

Other online methods

There are a number of other methods being used to run a profitable business online, but most are more specialized and expensive to develop. A few may be useful as part of your website:

Job openings. Many firms put listings of their job openings on their websites. This can lead to better recruiting by leading to more applicants and better targeting of applicants who have already been exposed to the company and can read company information on the website.

It's far better then a tiny, expensive ad in the Sunday paper. You can even set up your website to collect applications online, or to provide application forms online.

Customer service. Another profitable use of a website is providing customer service. Pages with frequently asked questions can give customers information 24 hours a day, seven days a week. (These pages are called FAQ pages.) When that fails, customers can complete an online form with their question, and you respond when your office reopens.

Several things make this work. Have your website send an immediate email response to your customer, telling them when to expect a response, and any other useful information. Then, check frequently and respond quickly to every request.

Finally, every question you receive should be added to your website with the answer so it can be used by other customers.

Some companies install a "bulletin board" on their website so customers can post questions, and those questions can be answered by other users and by you or your staff.

The bulletin board can be very useful, providing answers before you can get them answered and providing a dynamic "community" for your customers. The risk is that complaints are posted on your website and may be inflammatory. Most customers recognize this, but it may be something you'd rather avoid.

Publicity/public relations. Your internet website can be put to use maintaining communication with news media, analysts, and researchers who have an interest in your company.

Post pages with your company profile, history, reproducible photographs, maps, and recent press releases.

Use email capabilities to build and maintain your news release mailing list and to email the media as new releases are issued.

Disney maintains special websites for news media. They require registration, to keep a curious public out, but most companies will welcome the public to this information and make it accessible from their main website and other websites.

Directory. Associations of companies may want to provide a directory of members with contact information, providing an online referral service. This may be classified by business type or geographical location.

Survey customers and prospects. The internet is a great tool for surveying customers and prospects at very low cost. Results can be tabulated quickly, and those who have special needs may be identified and provided with quick customer service.

Content/Product delivery and subscriptions. Respectable content delivery is viable in some business lines. I know information providers who used to sell binders full of information and now sell that information online and deliver it instantly at virtually no delivery cost.

Many newspapers provide free access to their current issues but charge a fee to access archived stories online. The *Wall Street Journal* has charged for an online edition for a number of years, offering a substantial discount to subscribers of the hard-copy edition. Airlines sell etickets online, cutting their costs and simplifying purchases for their passengers.

Publishers of specialized information have had success selling ebooks online, though this has been slow to find success with books targeted to a general audience.

Corporate Stockholder Relations. If your company is publicly traded, use your website to maintain communication with current and potential stockholders.

Post pages with your company profile, history, annual reports, financial statements, and other public filings. Include a link to your press releases.

Teaching. Your websites can be used as an online "school" or training facility to teach guests how to use your products and services productively. You can also use online training for employee training and orientation to new products and policies.

Check Resources

www.InternetBusinessMagic.com
**Directory, Survey, Ecommerce, Product Delivery,
Teaching, Bulletin boards**

Do you need a big website?

Should you develop a big website, or a one-page sales letter? That's an issue that bounces around the internet community from time to time. There are proponents on both sides.

One side says you should have a comprehensive website that carries all your products and services, provides service and information, and establishes you as a business leader.

The other side says you should have "One-Page" websites that sell a single product with a lengthy sales letter, and not distract your potential buyer with everything else going on in your company.

The One-Page advocates make a good point, and show some success. And it certainly sounds easy. Frankly, it works best where they sell only one or a few products, where they don't develop much of a relationship with their customers, and where most of their marketing is through email newsletters and affiliates where they can promote one product with a simple domain name.

Since you're building a complete online business, and, like Disney, will rely on repeat business and referred prospects for growth and future profits, you want the comprehensive website.

However, the thought of creating a large, comprehensive website may seem daunting at this point.

Here's relief: You'll create a plan, then start developing your website one day at a time, one page at a time. When your first short page is done, you'll have a website that can start generating business in a small way.

How will your guests find your website?

I know people who put up an internet website and waited for people to come.

No one did.

This is one of the biggest challenges of the internet today, with millions of websites and hundreds of millions of people "surfing" the web, how do you get a buyer to come to your website and to make a purchase?

It comes down to promotion and guest retention.

What will you do to promote your website?

Disney has always been dedicated to promotion

Can you imagine Walt Disney building Disneyland and *not* telling anyone about it? Of course he told people about it. He told everyone he could get to listen. And he promoted it masterfully.

Disney has always been good with promotion. Probably because of a background in the movie business, Walt Disney was a good promoter. There are three keys to consider as you think about this.

Disney was *always* promoting. As Walt Disney was moving toward construction of Disneyland, he leveraged the young television industry with his library of film and film production abilities to get construction money.

Part of the deal, with the ABC television network, included a *weekly* hour-long television program, called *Disneyland*.

On this program, he regularly ran features about the construction of Disneyland. By the time Disneyland was ready to open, the public was eager to see it.

Disney was good at *Cross* Promoting. Attractions throughout the park were designed on the stories from Disney films. Some, like the Sleeping Beauty Castle, promoted films that hadn't yet been released.

The few exceptions, like Pirates of the Caribbean and The Haunted Mansion, were used as the basis for creating movies years later.

Roy Disney, Walt's brother, said, "We don't do anything in one line without giving a thought to its profitability in other lines."

You can do the same thing with your website and the rest of your business. Consider how to combine and package products and services, and to use one to lead to a sale of another.

In my business, my books on the Disney business model lead companies and associations to hire me to speak to their employees and conventions. Those meetings lead participants to buy my books and management systems.

Disney used publicity to the max. Publicity means all kinds of promotional effort. I usually narrow it a bit to mean "free advertising."

Walt was always having something new happening or opening at Disneyland, resulting in free mentions on radio and television, and in newspapers and magazines.

Today when you visit Disneyland or Walt Disney World, you may discover one or more radio stations are set up, broadcasting live from the streets of the theme park.

Your own promotion plan

To succeed, your website has to be "found." There are lots of ways for people to find you:

1. **Your own referrals.** You and your employees will refer people to your website, because it can provide information, ordering assistance, and support 24 hours a day.

2. **Advertising.** All current advertising should carry a reference to your website, just as it should carry your address and phone number. Some businesses will buy specific advertising to promote their website, but this is wasteful, since some customers would rather deal with you through traditional channels.

3. **Collateral materials.** Your sales and support materials should all promote your website, as should all stationery, business cards, and packaging materials.

4. **Newsletters.** Online newsletters are produced by thousands of companies and are a great source of referrals. If you offer certain useful information, they may give you a free link as part of a story related to your company. You can also write articles, and submit them to newsletters for publication in return for a link to your website. And many newsletters will take paid advertising, allowing you to buy a small ad with a link to your website.

5. **Articles.** Write articles for trade journals, small magazines, and newspapers that are read by your target market. Provide this service free in trade for a small note at the end of the article, like, "An expert on the Disney business model,

Rich Hamilton writes about marketing and customer service. More information at www.MagicStrategy.com."

6. **Other websites.** Get your website listed on other websites belonging to your organizations and associations, including groups like chambers of commerce, trade groups, marketing groups, and community groups where you are involved.

7. **Trade links with other websites.** That means you locate noncompetitive websites with material indicating their guests might have an interest in your website. A link is a bit of text or a button that, when clicked, opens up a window with new information, in this case, a different website. You make a deal with the other firm to put a link on their website that will pop their guests to your website. And you do the same at your website for them. Guests at one website who don't find what they want may have better luck at the other site. As a reciprocal trade, you should each get guests from the other.

8. **Press releases.** Put press releases on your website for newspapers, magazines, and broadcast media. The first place the media looks for information is the internet. When you post your press releases there, they can find you 24 hours a day from around the world, they can get key information, and they can contact you. This can result in interviews or opportunities for articles.

9. **Your own affiliate program.** Find other websites to promote your products or services and pay a commission. Suddenly the efforts of others will help build your business.

10. **Search engines.** Design your website to rank well with search engines, and sell to guests who find your website in that way. (The next chapter will help you do that.)

11. **Personal talks.** Become an "ambassador" for your company and speaking to local and regional Rotary, Kiwanis, or Lions clubs will carry your message to potential customers. Think of a useful "consumer message" that you can share with these community groups, and you've got the basis of a program.

This "short" list is really quite useful. What's important? Promote. Promote every way you can. Do it all. Do it *all*. And keep doing it.

Promote, promote, *promote!*

The "real" search engine strategy

It's important to recognize that while *people will find you* through search engines, most people will find you through the other methods listed in the last chapter.

What's a search engine?

Search engines are computers on the internet running software that reads most of the pages on most websites and catalogs or indexes the information so that someone can type a question or key phrase and get a list of links to websites with good, relevant information.

The first really big search engine was Alta-Vista. Later, Google became powerful, capturing the lion's share of the market. Still, there are many, probably hundreds, of other search engines. Some are run by major companies who would like to capture the majority of the search engine business.

When someone goes to a search engine website and types in a phrase that relates to your business, you'd like to show up, wouldn't you?

Yes! And you want to show up early in the listing, because some people never look past the first or second page of results.

What about those offers to submit your website to the top search engines?

There are hundreds, if not thousands, of services and products offering to "submit your website" to all the important search engines, and to "fix" your website so the search engines will give it a high ranking.

What I'm about to share with you is the one search engine method that works. It works well, and it works long-term.

It also makes sense.

First, what's wrong with all the services and software products that promise a good search engine ranking? *Plenty!*

They waste your money, because they don't work. The search engines are very complex computer programs that are constantly being changed to respond with links to the information their users want.

"Submitting" to search engines is a very simple process. You can do what you need to do in about ten minutes time. You do it once and never need to do it again, because the search engines figure out which websites change frequently and reload them accordingly.

They give you false hope, because you think you're going to get good results, then you don't. Or, maybe you get good results for awhile, then they stop.

They may even hurt your ability to get a good search engine ranking, because the search engines penalize sites that appear to be trying to "trick" them into a good ranking.

Here's the real secret!

When someone goes to a search engine website and types in a phrase (a "search phrase," sometimes called "search terms") that relates to your business, you want to show up. How can you make that happen?

Two things happen in concert when a search phrase is entered by a user. First, a list of websites that qualifies as a response for a particular query is compiled, then that list is sorted to rank the websites and put the list in order.

To rank well, you have to be selected *and* you have to rank well within that selection.

There are several "secret strategies."

1. Search phrase. First, you want to know what phrase or phrases your prospective customers are likely to type.

Shortly after my book, *Disney Magic: Business Strategy You Can Use at Work and at Home,* was published, I thought it would be great if my website would appear in the top ten if someone entered "Disney seminar" at leading websites. So I tried it at Google, and, sure enough, I was already showing up there, without doing anything special. It seemed like my lucky day!

Then I started wondering how often someone typed that phrase into a search engine.

I found a free, online service that answers that question, and learned that "Disney seminar" is *never* typed as a search phrase. (Well, certainly not often enough to matter.)

I was wrong! I needed to learn what phrases *were* being used!

So I queried on "Disney." I found a long list of search phrases with that word, including "Disney films," "Disney animation," and many, many others. But *none* of the terms had anything to do with business.

I'd already learned there is a strong interest in how Disney does business, but it's not a search phrase used at the search engines!

The conclusion? I needed to design my website so it would be found by the search engines in response to other search phrases. And that leads us to the second secret.

2. A high-content website. Create a website that has good, helpful information that will be of interest to someone who typed a query at a search engine.

The software engineers that are constantly changing and improving the search engines have an important goal in mind: They want the search engine to return good, relevant information for their users.

Even executives at search engine companies will tell you, "Design a comprehensive website loaded with useful information." After all, that's what they're looking for. Instead of trying to "trick" the search engines, create the kind of website they really want to find.

It's also what their users are looking for. And that means that when someone clicks through to your website, they'll stay because you gave them what they wanted. And your odds of a sale are increased as well.

3. Separate pages. Create a separate page on your website for each search engine phrase you want to hit.

I just told you about some of my key search phrases. If I want good results, I want to show up well for all those phrases.

I'll put a separate page on my website for each search phrase. Usually, each page will be a "feature article" that I've written, like you might find in a newspaper or trade journal. Occasionally, I can create a product or service description page that provides enough information it's likely to be found and ranked well by a search engine.

There are certain things I'll do to increase the odds that the search engines will recognize the page for what it is, and I'll list those on our website so you can get the latest information.

4. Links from other sites. Some key search engines rank you according to how often you are "linked to" from other websites. In its simplest form, that means that a search engine, like Google, will rank a website higher when it has more other websites that link to it.

Here's the catch: Google counts referrals from some websites as being worth more, and others may even lessen your ranking.

The lesson is simple. Make sure your website is listed at a number of other websites, particularly those related to you in a meaningful way, such as associations, trade groups, and vendor-customer websites.

5. Other search engines. Every search engine looks at other search engines when returning results.

When you get a good listing in one or two search engines, you'll suddenly start showing well in almost all search engines, even when you've never "submitted" your site to them.

One key site is a search engine that ranks your website based on editorial review. That means someone actually goes out to your website, reviews the information, decides whether or not to list it, and gives it a rating as to how good the information is. They probably also suggest categories and subject areas for searches.

A number of important fully automated search engines look at that one key site when determining how to rank results.

The lesson is simple; when your website is developed to the point that there's lots of good information available, submit to that website so their editors can evaluate your work. If it's good, you'll get a good ranking.

And if your website is lousy, you'll get a lousy rating, so don't submit to them until it's ready.

Here's the website: *www.dmoz.org* You'll want to submit each high-quality, high-content page to them for review.

Be sure to check our website before using this; if anything changes, we'll post the information there.

I was amazed when I first heard about search engines looking at each other, yet I've found it to be true. I've even read specifics about it in *The Wall Street Journal*.

The *Journal* pointed out that constantly changing dynamics in the industry, combined with mergers and acquisitions, result in changing dynamics with search engines, too. Here's another reason to check our website for the latest update to search engine technology. If I gave you the specific search engines where you need to submit, it might have changed by the time the book gets printed. At the website, I can keep the information up-to-date.

Directory websites

One of my biggest surprises came about a year after I first posted my website.

I ran a search engine search on my website name, and I had been listed in hundreds of "directory" websites, apparently used by some people looking up information.

I had never submitted to those directories, but I was there anyway. How did I get there?

When you follow the strategy I recommend in this book (and keep up-to-date on the website), the directories will find you. I don't know if many people use these directories, but search engines see them and it adds to the count of other websites that refer to you.

By the way, now several of those directories try to get me to personally "update" my listing, and pay a fee, to maintain my listing. I ignore them, and I recommend you ignore them, too.

What about pay-per-click search engines?

A few years ago, someone figured out that they could charge for search engine listings, and whoever paid the most would get listed at the top of the list.

This sounds like a great idea, and since thousands of people apparently use those search engines, a lot of people started bidding up the price to get a top-ranked listing. They pay anywhere from a few cents to a few dollars for each "click-through" when a user clicks to look at your website.

Generally, I discourage "advertising" like this. Here's why.

From the consumer's viewpoint, these search engines give lousy results, highly biased based on the payment of a few cents or dollars for a good listing.

Unless the websites with the "best" information were also bidding the most money, the search engine results are not very good.

The result is that the users either continue to use the site, blind to the fact that better results may be possible elsewhere, or they go elsewhere.

A variation on the idea returns "unbiased" results in the listing and adds targeted ads in an adjacent column. This is a better plan, because it maintains the integrity of the results, and at the same time offers advertisers special exposure. It also supports the search engine financially, and a good search engine is expensive to develop and run, so this benefits everyone.

Still, if you can get a good ranking for "free," why pay?

If you decide to try this kind of advertising, use all the power of the internet to make it work.

You can create special links to your website that, when used, increment a counter and establish tracking. That way you know how many of those people actually buy, what they buy, and how much they spend. (Our website will tell you how to accomplish this.)

Only then will you be able to determine how much to invest in this kind of advertising, and how much you can pay for each click-through.

If the "average" visitor to your website spends five dollars, and you have a fifty per cent margin, you net $2.50 for each visitor. That *might* mean you could pay *up to* $2.50 per click-through.

But you'll also want to track click-throughs by separate search phrases, because the results may vary.

For example, the "average" visitor who searched on "internet book" might spend three dollars, and the average visitor who searched on "internet profit" might spend seven.

Until you test it, you won't know.

This may be useful when you first get your website started, or when you first start building traffic. It can be frustrating waiting for directories and editor-driven search engines to list your website.

I still stand by my favorite thought on the issue: If you can get a good ranking for "free," why pay?

The website success cycle

Simply put, the process is this:

1. **Bring in lots of new guests to your website.** Use every available method. The previous chapter provides a list of useful promotion methods. Create a promotion plan and work that plan.

2. **Bring those guests back repeatedly.** For this, you have to create a relationship, fast!

3. **Convert guests to buyers.** Selling things people want, and providing them with the information they need to make the purchase. Make buying easy.

4. **Bring your buyers back to your website repeatedly.** Follow up every online sale with a sequence of support messages offering assistance, service, and gently suggesting additional products.

In the next chapter we'll cover creating a relationship with your website's guests and putting magic online.

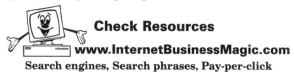

Check Resources
www.InternetBusinessMagic.com
Search engines, Search phrases, Pay-per-click

Odds are, they don't want to buy

When someone finds your web site, they probably have some kind of interest in your product or service.

But listen carefully. Odds are, they don't want to buy. Not now, anyway.

In traditional selling, this is *normal,* and the traditional salesperson knows that follow-up sales calls will be required to make the sale.

Even in retail, it's acceptable, because the prospective customer has found her way to the store, she is comfortable parking and coming into the store, and she can now find what she wants. It's easy to return.

But online, this normal circumstance is *death!* That's because even if they want to return when they *are* ready to buy (and *that day* probably *will* come), they won't know how to return to your website.

Even if they bookmark your web page (or add it to "Favorites") most people don't find the bookmark when the time comes. So they start over, and they find *someone else.*

There *is* a solution to this situation. It's called "Create a relationship... fast!"

Build and maintain a relationship... fast!

Remember the Disney idea, they want you to experience a magic moment!

You want the visitor to your website to experience several magic moments during their brief visit. As a result, you want them to give you their name and email address so you can stay in touch.

Since they won't be back otherwise, you've got to reach out to them.

Make the technology work for you

The beauty of the internet is that it's a bunch of computers connected together. When your guest visits your website, there are a number of thing you can do to build a relationship.

1. **Entertain them.** By providing articles, resources, charts, photographs, audio, video, and other useful information, you enter-

tain your guests, create credibility, and prepare them for an intelligent business relationship.

2. **Capture their email address.** One of your goals is to collect the email addresses of each guest, along with permission to mail to them. How do you do this? Create credibility and trust. Offer them something of value in return for their email address, and make it fun. You can offer gifts, online courses, ebooks, newsletters, and appropriate responses to inquiries.

3. **Sell them and follow-up.** Make it easy to buy from you online and provide an automated method to follow up after the sale with service, information, and gentle offers of additional products.

Let the technology work for you.

If you get an inquiry, you can respond by email within 24 hours. Then you can send a follow-up email every week, or once a month, to maintain a positive contact until they're ready to buy.

But it's better if you can set up your computer to do all that for you. They get their information faster. And it saves you a lot of work. Sure, sending an email is easy, but what will you do when you're getting several hundred email a week? How will you remember what to send to whom, and when? Let the computer do it. After all, that's the whole idea of the internet!

Your online newsletter

One of the easiest and most effective ways to build an ongoing relationship is an email newsletter that you write and mail once a month or so to maintain contact.

I know, you're thinking that you couldn't do that, because you're not a writer. But there's a solution. Read on.

Be sure to make your newsletter easy to read. Here are a few ideas to remember:

1. Base the newsletter on your compelling story or theme.
2. Articles can include success stories, observations, and stories about customers who had problems and used your products or services as part of a solution.
3. Include a short ad with a link to your website.
4. Make that link trackable so you can see how effective each newsletter is. (Our website lists hosting companies and services that will make your links trackable.)

Remember the goal is to create a relationship. Think of the stories and explanations you tell your friends and new acquaintances that help you build a friendship. Relate stories that help them solve problems using your product or service, or related subjects.

You can also get help writing the newsletter, by hiring a writer (or finding one among your staff) and telling them the stories you want in the newsletter each month. Often, you can find someone to do this through a local college or by calling a local newspaper, looking for a "freelance" writer. They write your stories and your newsletter goes out.

A friend of mine runs a business with no employees. Three years ago he started building his email list with about 100 names (his friends) and today, twice a month, he emails a newsletter to over 250,000 people. Many of them buy products from him occasionally for anywhere from $15 to $500 each. It works out to a dozen or more sales a day.

Hello! Did I get your attention yet?

Other automated processes

Lots of other processes can be automated on the internet, and your newsletter is only an example.

You can set up an inquiry form, and respond immediately with information by sending an email to the requestor. That email can include specific information and links to pages on your website to complete the information.

Then, the system can follow-up with a series of follow-up emails with additional information, reminders, and special offers, spaced at appropriate intervals.

Customers can be served with follow-up emails, thanking them for their purchase and offering customer service, supply items, and special sale values.

Certain products can include a series of useful information, emailed weekly or another appropriate interval.

Online courses can be offered, free or for a fee, that are delivered by a series of emails delivered daily or every other day.

Follow any of these with special "Bonus" articles, emails with useful special reports, news, and information.

When appropriate, you can provide information, training, and special programs through audio or video delivered by your website.

Many of these automated processes are delivered by a "sequential autoresponder," a software service that does all the technical work for you. It takes the requests, responds immediately, and follows up with the sequence of emails that you specify, and that helps built a valuable relationship.

More details on the current state of this technology will be found at our website, *InternetBusinessMagic.com*.

Check Resources

www.InternetBusinessMagic.com

Newsletters, Autoresponders, Audio, Video

Sell what they want, not what they need

The old analogy about selling refrigerators to Eskimos was stupid. Why would you try? When you could sell them something they want and need?

Okay, those who know are aware that Eskimos need and want refrigerators as much as anyone. They live in houses, just like most people.

But the point is clear. Rather than trying to sell something people don't want (or something they don't know they want), sell something they want.

One consultant I know says it this way. If you're going to make money online, sell something people are already buying online.

That's because it's expensive to try to invent something new and convince people that they want it and that they're safe buying it online.

When I tell my story about going online to buy grease for my garage door opener, people laugh. But when I did it, all I could find at the hardware store was an expensive, tiny tube of grease. I searched online, and found what I wanted. Same price, 10 times the grease. That's what I wanted!

Sell something people want. The best test of that is that they're already buying it online. That proves they want it. It proves they're willing to buy it online. And it proves they're already looking online to buy it.

You don't want to invent the market.

The successful exceptions have been spectacular. eBay may be the best example, as they successfully created the online auction market. Others who have tried to copy them have been far less successful. eBay made a market, and they own the "franchise" in the mind of the public. It cost them *a lot* of money to accomplish that, and it was a high risk investment.

So don't try to create an entirely new market on the internet.

On the other hand, you don't want to sell *exactly* what someone else is selling. That makes you a "me, too" seller, and makes it a price fight.

Bundle it, redesign it, or rename it to make it better and unique in the marketplace.

Figure out who is buying online, and what they want, and sell them that.

Write it to sell it

I'm always running into people who say they can't write anything, and that becomes their excuse for not doing anything. I need to give you a few suggestions.

First, you *can* write. *And you must!*

You don't have to write a lot, it doesn't have to be perfect, and you can have help, either writing or fixing what you wrote.

Along with the thought that you need to offer things that people want, I'd like to suggest you can write simple, "to the point" copy that will *link their want* with your product.

All your copy, whether it's an article for your newsletter or a sales "letter" describing one of your products, should have a purpose. And toward that purpose, you want people to think:

1. "I want that product."
2. "I want it right now."
3. "This is the only place I can get it."

I recommend formulating your copy according to the *Benefit-Sell* ad format. It starts with a "benefit statement," an offer that declares what you will do for or give your reader.

Then you make the offer, provide details that prove the worth of the product, offer testimonials and credibility facts, restate the offer and ask for the desired action.

A big vocabulary—ouch!

Write your copy like you talk. No one wants to read flowery "intellectual" text. And if you talk with flowery, intellectual language, *quit it!*

Your English teacher wanted you to have a big vocabulary, but you're not selling to English teachers. By using that fancy vocabulary you will lose business fast!

Additional learning materials are available to help you learn that method. And you can hire someone who *is* a writer to go through your writing and clean up the grammar, spelling, punctuation, and language.

Check Resources
www.InternetBusinessMagic.com
Writing copy

Selling products through affiliate programs

Affiliate programs are real "magic." An online vendor agrees to pay a commission, or referral fee, to other website operators who refer their visitors to the vendor. There is payment only when a sale is made.

Part of the beauty of this kind of program is that it can work both ways. You can sell others' products by becoming their affiliate and referring business to them. And you can expand your own sales by finding your own affiliates who will refer their guests to you.

What to sell?

What if you don't have a product to sell? Get one.

Ohmigosh! That sounds flippant! And I don't mean it to be.

Not long ago, my friend Rick approached me for help. He had recently been injured on the job, and he needed to put together something he could use to start building an income, even with a back injury that might keep him out of work forever.

Unlike an existing business, Rick didn't have anything ready to sell. *He needed more than a website. He needed a product.*

Lots of people like Rick are searching for ways to make money on the net. They want something that is risk-free and requires no financial investment. Some have very little Web experience and others are extremely knowledgeable. Their time "availability" can range from hours to full days.

The best product is one with high value that is unique to you, as opposed to a name-brand product that is available from lots of other firms. The reason is simple. If possible, you don't want to be competing with other firms, especially online companies, on price alone.

One way to solve the problem is to create a quality information product, based on some kind of information you already know, have available, or can easily come by, and that has *high value* to others who *don't* know what you know. *Sounds impossible?* Not as tough as you might think. The trick is knowing a few secrets about how to approach the project.

Referring your guests to others for fun and profit

The other way to have a product is selling someone else's product. For Rick, and others like him, that means a *quality* affiliate program.

Of course, paying a commission or referral fee isn't unique to the internet. What is unique is that it's so easy to set up. Once a vendor is set up with the proper software, all you have to do is sign up (this should be free), and the vendor's website will give you code for links on your website so your guests can jump to the vendor's website, make a purchase, and add a small amount to your next commission check.

The technical part is easy, because most of it is handled by the vendor's computer.

The practical side is a bit more complex. You'll want to choose programs that relate to your website's theme or story. And you want to be sure you're referring your guests to a reliable company.

At our MagicStrategy.com website, we refer guests to a variety of books about Disney. These can all be purchased online, and we earn a small commission.

Check our online information for more about choosing affiliate partners.

Selling your product through affiliates

One of the most powerful tools at your disposal is setting up your own referral or affiliate program. Others affiliate with you and refer their guests to your website. You pay a referral commission for any business you receive from your affiliates.

Once your website is set up to handle affiliate sign up and to track their business, it's up to you to promote the idea. You want to attract "quality" affiliates who will drive lots of interested guests to your website. Give them help on your website to make it easy to promote you, including ads, articles, and other suggested copy.

Then it's up to you to convert those into sales, profiting both you and your affiliate.

The *best way* is probably doing *both:* Find or create your own profitable products to sell, *and* sell someone else's products through an affiliate program. The affiliate program would give you something to sell to start, while you're creating a product to sell. When your own product is ready, you add it to your website and *generate income both ways.*

Check Resources
www.InternetBusinessMagic.com
Creating product, Affiliate programs

Guestology closes the loop

Following a performance of *Disney's Aladdin—A Musical Spectacular* at Disney's California Adventure, I watched as four or five Disney cast members approached guests leaving the Hyperion Theatre.

The guests were asked three or four questions, and the answers were entered into portable tablet computers. "Please tell us how you liked the show," one asked. "Rate it from one to five, where one is not very much and five is excellent..."

Disney calls this "guestology." It's their proactive way to find out how their customers feel about what's happening.

They also take comment forms at various guest relations locations, and Disney cast members are trained to listen for comments about how a guest's vacation is going, and to even ask about it in order to learn what's happening.

A server in a restaurant might hear about a problem in the town square. That comment is passed on to a supervisor who calls the appropriate manager to make a quick correction.

In other firms it might be called market research, or consumer research, and it might be left for the marketing department to review at a convenient time.

At Disney, it's personal. They review this input constantly, and adjust operations accordingly. The principle is "evaluate and adapt." It allows for instant course correction.

In your online business, it can be hard to evaluate what's happening with your customers, since you don't see them face-to-face.

That makes it even more important to survey your customers to find out how they feel about your products, your services, and your company.

This can be accomplished with formal online surveys, simple follow-up email messages asking for comments, survey forms included in shipments and with invoices, and with specific telephone surveys to make sure they're happy.

Sometimes, you'll hear from them anyway. Today, as I'm writing this, I received an email from a customer that said, "Hi, just wanted to let you know I received the book today! Thank you so much!!"

That's a good hint that I'm doing well, but it would be better to get a little more information. Four to six simple questions is plenty. A longer survey frustrates customers. A survey postcard might say:

Thanks for your business!
We really want to know how you feel about your experience with our company. Please rate the following on a scale of one to five, with one being poor and five being excellent:

	Poor				Excellent
Product	1	2	3	4	5
Product condition	1	2	3	4	5
Delivery Time	1	2	3	4	5
Packaging	1	2	3	4	5
Website	1	2	3	4	5
Ordering Process	1	2	3	4	5

Additional Comments:

You could add a line for their name, or code their order number onto the card or survey form. If it's a mail-in form, be sure to pay the postage.

Finally, be sure to thank those who participate, and take action on the results. Your customers will appreciate the recognition, and they'll be impressed when they see changes that take place based on their comments.

 **Check Resources**
www.InternetBusinessMagic.com
Surveys

Collect testimonials

Entertainer Julie Andrews said, "One memory I'll cherish forever is the thrill of seeing the Magic Kingdom for the first time and guess who my tour guide was? Walt Disney!"

Supreme Court Justice Earl Warren said, "Everywhere I travel in the world people ask me about Disneyland!"

Danny Kaye said, "You're never too old or never too young to enjoy the magic of the Magic Kingdom."

In 1960, Herman Wouk, author of *The Winds of War,* said, "I don't blame [Nikita] Krushchev for jumping up and down in rage over missing Disneyland. There are few things more worth seeing in the United States, or indeed anywhere in the world."

The official Disneyland Guest Book lists hundreds of presidents, vice presidents, prime ministers, kings, queens, crown princes, princes, princesses, senators, supreme court justices, governors, ambassadors, sultans, emperors, astronauts, cosmonauts, celebrities, and famous athletes.

These testimonials, and the names from the guest book, are taken from an official Disneyland media kit. It's part of the story Disney wants told. "It's fun to go to Disneyland!"

In the early years of Disneyland, Walt Disney was often photographed with celebrity guests. Experienced in the art of publicity, Walt knew that it helped get free publicity, and provided a credible endorsement of his biggest project.

Testimonials do not have to be from famous people. In fact, the best testimonials come from your customers!

When you're operating offline, testimonials are a powerful part of your selling tools. They create credibility, provide suggestions on the use and satisfaction of using your products, and help your customer feel safe in making a purchase. Online, that's even more important.

There are several keys to collecting testimonials. It's not a big secret how. The trick is implementing it as a plan, rather than hoping it will happen.

Be worthy

If you want testimonials from your customers, the first principle is to be "worthy." That means you need to provide a quality product or service, and provide a real value. You need to deliver it quickly and professionally.

Of course, this is important to the success of your business overall, and it's especially important when you're asking for a testimonial.

When you ask a customer for a testimonial, you want them to think, "Sure, I'd be happy to have my name associated with this company and this product."

What you *don't* want is for them to think, "This was a piece of junk, how can I recommend it?" or, "They lost my order and I complained three times, and now they want a testimonial? Hah!"

Make it a priority

Most companies deserve far more testimonials than they get, because they haven't made it a priority.

If you make it a priority, you will get the testimonials you deserve.

Make it part of your business system. Include a request for a testimonial in every package you ship. Email a request to customers after they buy from you. Make it part of a follow-up survey.

Offer a gift to everyone who responds, whether it's a positive, usable testimonial, or not. Most will be, and you will gain the feedback you need, along with a bunch of good testimonials.

Ask, ask, ask

As you make this part of your system, remember this last principle. It's not a onetime effort. Make it part of your continuing system. Ask and keep asking.

You need and deserve these testimonials. Go after them!

Make it easy to buy

Some people have never made a purchase online. "I'm afraid of getting ripped off," one friend told me. "How do I know I'll get what I order?"

"Most credit card companies protect you against online fraud," I explained.

But it's up to you, with an online business, to overcome the fears of your guests.

Reverse the risk with a guarantee

Testimonials and referrals help your guest feel secure about making a purchase. But there's still an element of concern. Sometimes it's as simple as, "What if I don't like the color?" or, "What if it's too small?"

A money back guarantee is your best friend. Assuring a buyer's satisfaction "or your money back" is the best way to provide your guest with ultimate confidence in doing business with you. Promote it on your website. Only a very few will take advantage of you unfairly. Sears and Amway have proven it over the years; the costs are far outweighed by the benefits.

Lee Cockerell, Executive Vice President of Walt Disney World Operations, says it this way, "Do what's 'right.' It's hard to get in trouble if you decide in favor of the guest."

Credit cards make the money flow

Years ago, "mail order" was hampered by the need to wait for orders, with payment, mailed to the mail order company. Credit cards and toll-free numbers changed that, and the business boomed. It's even more important on the internet, with an international market.

A huge percentage of internet business is done with credit cards. You simply must have a way to take major credit cards. It's pretty easy; more details are available at our website.

Check Resources
www.InternetBusinessMagic.com
Credit Cards

Section 3: Implementation

Who should plan your internet business, and how?

Who should plan your internet business? You!

As I write this, I don't know if you're an individual running or wanting to start a small business, or a corporate executive.

If you're part of a corporation, I don't know if you're the CEO, a vice-president in charge of marketing or technology, or a retail line manager. Maybe you're a management hopeful, thinking that developing an online business could propel you to a better job or a better career.

Frankly, it doesn't matter. The answer is the same: *You.*

Here's why. You've taken the time to read this book and that demonstrates a desire to make something successful happen online. You care more than anyone else.

If you have the resources to delegate this project, and you delegate it, you'll never learn the powerful nuances that make a successful internet business prosper.

You already have a product or service. (If you don't, I have a few suggestions on that, too, later.)

Marketing is the key, along with a proper strategy for developing your business website.

You probably already know how to sell your products and services. You need to translate it to a set of web pages, and add electronic purchase or inquiry capability. And you'll want to learn how to promote using online resources.

How do you put it together? That's what's next.

So, take on the planning function yourself, and drive this project to success.

Later, you may find you can delegate much of it to specialists in your company. But for now, do it yourself.

Is your website 'Under Construction?'

If you've spent any time on the internet, you've probably come across those "Under Construction" messages. Those are put up by companies who are admitting that they haven't taken the time to finish a page (or pages) on their website.

It's really a stupid message, because *every* website is under construction. Even Disneyland.com, one of Disney's well established websites, is under construction. You won't find an "Under Construction" message on the Disneyland.com website, though.

Every good website is undergoing change, improvement, and redesign. So a website is never done.

Disneyland is always changing

Walt Disney said, "Disneyland will always be building and growing and adding new things... new ways of having fun, of learning things and sharing the many exciting adventures which may be experienced here."

That's a pretty good description of a good business website, too.

And it's a relief when you're getting started with a new website. Because your website can begin with just one short page. Then, twice a week you can add another page, and in three short months you'll have a 27-page website.

Of course, your pace may be faster, or slower. That's up to you. The key is that you can do it one step at a time.

You'll never be "under construction." Or, depending on how you look at it, you'll *always* be under construction.

Walt said, "Disneyland is like a piece of clay. If there's something I don't like, I'm not stuck with it. I can reshape and revamp... Whenever I go on a ride, I'm always thinking of what's wrong with the thing and how it can be improved."

It's a good attitude for you to adopt towards your website.

You'll always be finding ways to improve it and make it more fun, more informational, more adventurous.

A later chapter will give you a specific plan for creating your internet business and website. Before you start that, you need a written business plan.

A Disney project planning secret

Walt Disney and his staff developed a very useful tool for project planning in the early 1930s when they were planning animated films. It's called *storyboarding,* and it's explained in a little more detail in *Disney Magic: Business Strategy You Can Use at Work and at Home.*

Disney used drawings pinned to four by eight foot fiber boards for those early storyboards. The drawings could easily be rearranged to change the presentation of the story, making planning and revisions easy.

Later, because the Disney staff was used to planning this way, they applied the principle to other projects using index cards and pins to attach them to fiber boards.

Today, it's easier to use self-stick notes, and lay them out on a large piece of cardboard or paneling. Small projects, including the initial planning for your website, can probably be organized with small two or three-inch self-stick notes and an 11x17 inch piece of cardboard. The moveable self-stick note sheets make it easy to reorganize and rearrange everything.

For your internet business plan, I suggest using full sheets of notebook paper or sheets from a legal pad. Each sheet will be used to design one part of your website. Then you can arrange them in storyboard fashion by arranging them on a bulletin board or even on a large table, like a conference table or dining table. The arrangement will allow you to organize the project, and your website, in a logical fashion.

I've looked at many so-called "storyboarding" software programs, and have yet to find one that provides the flexibility and visual cues for planning that you get with index cards or self-stick notes. Many of the software programs are wonderful for presenting ideas, but not for reorganizing or planning projects.

Your internet business plan in an hour

Every project needs a plan, and your internet business is no exception. While you will build your website one page at a time, one day at a time, your success will come about because you have planned and strategized your entire internet business in advance.

While I'm endorsing planning, let me stress one point. I don't believe you need to create a *comprehensive long term plan*. That's a project itself, and might take months. You might want to do that after you get started, but it's more important to get started and get your internet business in place.

I'm suggesting you find a quiet place where you won't be interrupted. I like to use a restaurant in my neighborhood where it's quiet in mid-afternoon. You can write out a simple plan in an hour or less. Then you can visit with business associates about it, if you wish, and revise or adjust the plan slightly.

I'm going to give you a list of things to include in your plan. For most of these, write only a paragraph, or a few paragraphs. To get this done in an hour, you have to be brief. And don't worry about being a great writer; what's important here is having a great plan.

By starting today, your plan can be done tomorrow!

First things first: Outcomes

The first step in planning your internet business is writing down the outcomes you expect from your online business.

Do you expect to sell products? What products?

Do you expect to sell services? What services?

Will you sell directly on the internet, or generate leads to be followed up in person?

Are you going to use your website to assist in making sales presentations?

Will you promote products offered on other websites?

Will you have an affiliate program so others can refer customers to your website and receive a commission?

Do you want any additional website functions, like job openings, customer service, public relations, customer surveys, stockholder relations, or training? How do you want to implement these ideas?

Do you expect to develop any additional websites for special purposes or for different parts of the company?

Your compelling story

What will you use as your compelling story to entice your website's guests into looking through your information?

You might think of this as a theme, and the most effective theme will relate to some kind of story. The story does not have to be complex or fantasy-related, like some Disney stories. It just needs to be compelling, or interesting, to your guests.

Think about what they might be concerned about, or what they might want to use to improve their business, make their job easier, help their family, or put fun in their life.

Our *InternetBusinessMagic.com* website is based on a simple theme: "Build an internet business using the magic strategy demonstrated by Walt Disney when he created Disneyland and Walt Disney World."

Your opt-in newsletter

Remember how most guests to your website are not ready to buy? You need to have a way to build a relationship with them over time so that when they are ready, they will come to you.

Sadly, on the internet most websites are quickly forgotten. Even if a guest bookmarks your site, they may not find it when they're ready to buy.

When a guest signs up for your free, *opt-in* newsletter, they have invited you to mail them your newsletter regularly, at least, until they ask you to stop. That gives you the opportunity to continue to feed them useful information and stories of interest, related to your theme.

Opt-in means that they requested being on your list, at your website, at a meeting, by mail or phone; it was *their* option.

What short articles will you include in an opt-in newsletter in order to build a relationship with customers and prospects? How often will you mail your newsletter?

What will you call it? Related to your theme, what will you promise about your newsletter that will entice your guests to sign up?

Other automated processes

What other automated processes do you want on your website? Sequential email courses, inquiry follow-up, and customer service processes may be designed for a sequential autoresponder system.

Promotion

How will you promote your website?

Jot down a few paragraphs about how you will promote your website. Remember, this does not have to be expensive. Look back over the materials on promotion, advertising, and publicity.

Delivery

How will you deliver your products and services? Where will you deliver? Are you limited geographically to a local area, to a state or country, or can you deliver worldwide?

What methods will be used? Some software and information products can be delivered online, but most require inventorying, packing, and shipping.

There are probably limits to how much business you can handle. What are the limits, and how will you deal with that?

Write a few paragraphs to answer these questions. Then you can move on to planning the website to make it happen.

How your website is organized

Finally! It's time to look at the actual website plan.

A website is a collection of "pages."

A page is a set of images and text, seen on a computer screen. Often, the page is longer (and even wider) than the screen, and you may have to scroll through the page in order to see it all. Occasionally a page is extremely long, and might take 10, 15, or more sheets of paper if you printed it on your printer.

A "link" on a page is a section of text, an image, or a button that has been programmed to load a new page on your computer when it is "clicked" with the mouse. The new page may be part of your website or a page on another website. Some links actually launch a special program on the website that creates a special page, casts a vote, subscribes to a newsletter, or some other special function.

Make your products easy to find and easy to buy.

Plan each page on a separate piece of paper. (Each sheet will be a "page;" that should be easy to remember!)

Planning your web pages

Your web pages should be "user friendly." Make them easy to understand, and easy to use. Use links and buttons that make sense. Call them "Articles," not "Old musings."

There are several pages every website should have. Take a sheet of paper and write the page name across the top. Here are the first pages you want to design:

Home page. I like to call your "home page" the "welcome page," because it's often the first page a guest sees and provides the greeting and introduction to your overall theme or story. It's like the front entrance to a store, providing access to other areas of the store, or website.

Every website *must* have a home page. Plan it first, and be aware that it will probably change often.

On your Home Page planning sheet write a short description of what you will say to introduce your theme or compelling story.

Then make a note about a few news items, featured products, or special services that you want to feature first on your home page.

Your home page and *every* page should have a small sign-up form for your newsletter. Include your address and phone number at the bottom of each page, too.

Finally, make a list of navigation "buttons" that you'll use to direct guests to various sections of the website. Think of this as a list of departments or sections. Typical buttons might be Products, Services, Articles, About Us, and Contact Us. These buttons are normally arranged along the left margin, and are duplicated on all pages of the website to allow for quick navigation from any page.

Each button will direct a guest to a different page on your website.

Now, continue by designing pages for each section:

About Us page. This page is a short profile about your company and key people who help define the company. Remember, a lot of the people who visit your website know nothing about you. This allows you to start creating a relationship with anyone who is concerned about who they might be doing business with. A short history and a few stories give you an opportunity to bring a guest up to date and give you more credibility than an offline firm is likely to share.

Contact Us page. *Every* page should have minimal contact information on it, and a Contact Us page should have all kinds of contact information for customers or prospects who need to get in touch with you.

List your physical and mailing address, key email addresses, phone numbers, and fax numbers.

Provide direct numbers for ordering and for customer service, and make it easy for someone to email you.

Some search engines rank you higher for having a complete Contact Us page, so be sure to have one, even though you think every page already has this covered.

Products page. Your products page should lead guests to information and purchase buttons for each product you sell.

Each product should have a separate page, with picture, sales information, and purchase button. It's a sort of online "sales brochure."

If you sell only one product, your Products page will be the page for that one product.

If you have a limited number of products, list the products on your Products page, with a small description and, if there's room, a small picture.

If your catalog is larger, you will list departments, and each department will link to lists of the department's products.

Some firms prefer a separate Products page for each department with navigation buttons along the side that lead to those pages. If you choose this route, plan a separate page for each department.

With thousands, or even hundreds, of products, you reach a point where you may decide a database should be created to list products, allowing for a search function to locate the proper products. Check our website for current information; this may require the services of a database designer or special ecommerce server.

Services page. Similar to a Products page, your Services page lists services you offer.

This may be one or multiple pages depending on the variety of services you offer.

Articles page. The easiest way to add quality content to your website is to create a series of articles, each on an important topic related to your offerings.

Your Articles page has a listing for each article, probably with a short description and a link to the pages with specific articles.

Plan articles you think will be of particular importance to your guests. Later, as you wrap up your plan, you will want to create an article for each search phrase you want search engines to respond to.

Initially, you will want to create three or four articles to post on your website. Over time, you will expand this gradually.

Some individual articles might link to additional detail pages.

As you do your plan, create a sheet for the Articles page and for each individual article.

Other pages

You may want special interest links at the bottom of the page as well.

There is a great need for material mor newspapers, magazines, and broadcast media. The first place they look is on the internet. Give them a reason to interview you.

On my website, I put links for *news media* looking for information, photographs, and news releases, and for *meeting planners,* who may need information or photographs to promote my appearance at a convention or meeting. You may have similar or different needs.

There are a number of utility pages you will want to plan for your website.

Privacy Policy page. A simple Privacy Policy assures people you're not harvesting their email addresses to sell to spammers. When someone signs up for your newsletter, or buys a product, they want assurance that you're not going to ruin their email inbox.

Terms of Use page. A Terms of Use page is a similar "legal document" specifying that you own the copyright to the information on the website and under what terms a guest gets to use the website and information. Most guests won't read these pages, but you are afforded at least some protection and you establish ownership to your own material.

Visit major websites to see the kind of information that is typically used. Also check the links at *InternetBusinessMagic.com*.

Typical website organization

The Home page links to other pages, which link to other pages. It's a hierarchical organization of pages, much like a company's organization chart. The organization of a website might be drawn something like that in Diagram A.

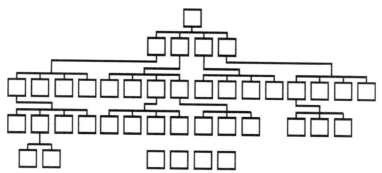

Diagram A. Typical website organization

Organizing your own website

Go back through each page you've planned and think about what each should contain. You may want to jot down:

1. The story or key information for that page
2. A list of the links from that page to more detailed information
3. A list of links from that page to related pages in your website
4. Any photograph or special image that you want to include

As you plan, draw a diagram or organization chart reflecting your specific design.

Remember, this plan is supposed to be done in an hour, so keep it brief!

Search engine strategy

As you finish your basic design, go to our special website and find the tools for finding search phrases. You can refer back to the chapter on search engines for details.

Make a list of search phrases that you expect customers to use to find your website.

Now, go back to your website diagram and add article pages or other pages that can be used to satisfy each of the search phrases.

Finished? Great! Now you're ready to move from plan to *action!*

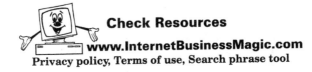

Check Resources
www.InternetBusinessMagic.com
Privacy policy, Terms of use, Search phrase tool

Who should build your website?

If you're the president of Amazon.com or Walmart, you'll be turning this over to your IT department and can expect a sizeable investment and considerable delay. (And you should still read the rest of this book, and share it with your IT people.)

Small and medium-sized firms have an interesting option.

Do it yourself. *Gasp!*

My web designer friends hate me for telling you this!

Before you skip on, let me make this clear. There is an easy way to do it yourself, and to do it well. I'll get to that in a moment. First, understand why:

Only you really know what you need to do to sell your product or service. You probably do it every day.

When you get new information, or a new idea, and you want it on your website, you want it to happen immediately. Most web designers take a long time to respond. If you handle it yourself, you can do it.

When you're out of town, and you come up with something that should be on your website, you want to be able to add it. You want to be able to pull out your notebook computer, or go to an "internet cafe" where you use their computer to easily update your website. Right now!

And remember your opt-in email newsletter for customers and prospects who request it so that you can stay in touch. In exchange for a little useful news or information, you get to stay in the "top of mind" with them and you also get a chance to sell something. You don't want to pay much for the privilege. Again, you want your website to do most of the work and you want to manage this easily by yourself.

I've known plenty of people who hired expensive contractors to develop their websites. Some ended up with beautiful websites. All were frustrated because they had no control.

Trust me on this. *You want control.*

You can do this the easy way, or the hard way. It's your choice. Easy or hard?

The hard way

Domain name. You can go register your own domain.

Hosting server. Then you can search for a hosting company to host your website. This is the company whose computer "servers" actually contain your computer files and "serve" them to your internet guests. If you try this, you'll immediately discover the huge number of options available.

How much bandwidth do you need? What are the monthly transfer limits? How much storage do you really need? Do you need MySQL? What about cgi? Don't forget FTP. Do you need a server running NT, Linux, OpenBSD, or FreeBSD? And this is just the beginning.

Software. Now you need to choose which software will be best for your company to design the web pages. There are several major packages. Would Microsoft FrontPage do the job, or should you get NetObjects Fusion, Macromedia Dreamweaver, or Adobe GoLive? Will it work on the server you leased?

Training. How do you learn to use the software? How do you create the pages? Do you need to be able to write HTML code? How do you FTP your web pages to your website?

It's no wonder that people delegate all this to someone else, and pay thousands of dollars to contractors to do it all for them. It's even worth it.

Except, it's not necessary.

The easy way

Do you have to conquer the technical challenge? No! Today, there's a solution to the problem. You're not the first person to be troubled by all the complicated procedures.

Most websites can be created and maintained, by you, directly online.

The key is to find a hosting company that provides a comprehensive online website development package. (They all say they do, but they don't.)

At our website, I'll show you how to make it happen.

I've located some easy, free online courses that you can use to get a great education on internet marketing. And I have the answer to how you go through the mechanics of putting a business website together.

Check Resources

www.InternetBusinessMagic.com

Hosting companies, Tracking, Autoresponders

It's easy, one day at a time!

Once you've established your foundation, and come to grips with the nature of the business, it's time to get started on the website itself.

Build your website one day at a time, one page at a time.

When you're only partially done, you'll have a working website!

Here's an outline of what to do to get the job done without becoming overwhelmed by the task:

1. Write up your business plan (in one hour).
   - What do you want the website to do for you? List your desired outcomes.
   - Your overall theme, told in the form of a compelling story.
   - Advertising, publicity, and promotion.
   - Delivery systems
   - Your website plan
   - Design your hierarchical website structure. (organization chart)
   - Compile a list of search engine phrases you're going to "chase." (See *InternetBusinessMagic.com* for the search phrase suggestion tools.) Add a page for each of these to your plan.
2. Sign up with the hosting company.
   (See *InternetBusinessMagic.com* for hosting information.)
3. Download and read the hosting company instructions so you gain further understanding of how they work to help you build a successful website.
4. Create your front page, welcoming guests and introducing them to your compelling story. *Now you have a small, working website!*

5. Create pages for About Us, Contact Us, Privacy Policy, and Terms of Use.

6. Create an opt-in newsletter. Put a small signup form on your front page and write the first newsletter that will go out to new subscribers. (This form should be designed to go on *every* page.)

7. Create a catalog or selling page with several products.

8. Create "sales presentation" or brochure pages.

9. Create lead generation pages.

10. Create an Articles page, listing a couple of interesting articles. Link those to pages that have the full text of the articles.

11. Add search engine pages, probably to your articles list, each page designed to gather responses to a different search engine phrase.

12. Create pages that refer to other websites, if that's part of your plan.

Now you've got an active website. Continue to develop it by adding and updating products, articles, and presentation materials. And change your front page occasionally to keep it fresh, with brief messages directing visitors to new information and current promotions.

Write and send your newsletter monthly, and watch the business grow.

What if you already have a website?

How is it doing?

As you've read this book, you've discovered new strategies, new methods, and new uses for your website.

Now, redesign and redevelop your new, more powerful website.

It will be easier because you can borrow the good things from your old site. You will have the best of both!

Let's roll...

Help along the way

Since this book is intentionally thin, so that it's quick to read and easy to carry with you, it's necessary to provide you with additional resources to assist in your endeavors. I'm excited to be able to do that in a dynamic and adaptive way.

The *InternetBusinessMagic.com* website gives you specific resources that relate to the internet. But that's not enough. I want to stay in touch with you and help you achieve all your dreams, your goals, your desires. I also want you to share with me your success stories and let you read the stories of others. For this purpose we have created another special internet website, shared by readers of all the Magic Strategy series of books:

www.MagicStrategy.com

To access the special section for readers who have finished the book click on the "Members" button. Your special access code is 1955. If you've paid close attention, you'll remember the significance of that number, and that's why we used it as an access code.

Much of what I've shared with you here is good business strategy for any business, online and offline. Most of it is relatively simple.

It's in your hands now

As I've discussed this material with others, we recognized that many people will read it and ignore it, or read it and go on about trying to create an online business without drafting business plans, defining service themes and core purposes, or creating compelling stories to provide overall themes for their websites. Please take responsibility to see that you're not in this group.

As you've read the material here, you've gained the methods and resources you need to effectively put your business online. It may seem complex, but once you get started, things will move pretty fast.

It's always interested me to listen to people tell me they haven't had time to write a simple business plan or project plan, and they take longer explaining their woes than it would take to write the plan.

Take a late lunch at a quiet coffee shop and start your plan today. With this book, you know how.

Share this information with others in your family, your company, your school, or your organization. As more people adopt these methods, the resulting synergy will create remarkable results.

A lesson from the beavers

Walt Disney said, "Everyone needs deadlines. Even the beavers. They loaf around all summer, but when they are faced with the winter deadline, they work like fury. If we didn't have deadlines, we'd stagnate."

Set a deadline for getting your business working on the internet.

You need several things to succeed in this business, and it all begins with a good business plan.

Sell something people want.

Get very good at driving guests to your websites.

Get even better at converting those guests to buyers.

Make it fun to buy from you so they want to come back and buy again and again.

You now have all the information and tools you need to put together your own online business.

Read this book several times. Use the appropriate chapters as you work through the various tasks.

After you're up and running, read the book again to see what new ideas you find. And check back at our website occasionally for new technology and updated information as we find it.

With what you've learned here, you no longer have an excuse.

Do it.

Suggested Reading

Books and Audio

Adventures in Creative Thinking, audio by Mike Vance

Be Our Guest, book by the Disney Institute

Disney Magic: Business Strategy You Can Use at Work and at Home, book by Rich Hamilton

Disney Magic Ideabook: Using Disney's Magic Strategy for Your Own Business Success, book by Rich Hamilton

The Disney Version, book by Richard Schickel

The Disney Way, book by Bill Capodagli and Lynn Jackson

Inside the Dream: The Personal Story of Walt Disney, book by Katherine Barrett, Richard Greene, and Katherine Greene

Inside the Magic Kingdom: Seven Keys to Disney's Success, book by Tom Connellan

The Magic Kingdom: Walt Disney and the American Way of Life, book by Steven Watts

The Man Behind the Magic: The Story of Walt Disney, book by Katherine Greene and Richard Greene

Mouse Tales: A Behind the Ears Look at Disneyland, book by David Koenig

Prince Of The Magic Kingdom: Michael Eisner And The Re-Making Of Disney, book by Joe Flower

Remembering Walt: Favorite Memories of Walt Disney, book by Amy Boothe Green and Howard E. Green

Walt Disney, book by Diane Disney Miller as told to Pete Martin

Walt Disney: An American Original, book by Bob Thomas

Walt Disney: Famous Quotes

Walt Disney Imagineering: A Behind the Dreams Look at Making the Magic Real, book by The Imagineers and C. E. Jones

Internet Resources

Disney Online: http://www.disney.com

Disneyland Inside & Out: http://www.intercotwest.com

Laughing Place: http://laughingplace.com

MiceAge: http://www.miceage.com

Mouse Planet: http://www.mouseplanet.com

Mike Vance: http://www.creativethinkingassoc.com

Special websites for readers of this book:
    http://www.InternetBusinessMagic.com
    http://www.MagicStrategy.com

Index

About the Author

Rich Hamilton writes and speaks on customer service, selling, leadership, and business strategy. A former broadcast executive and newspaper reporter, Rich also has experience as a professional photographer and systems analyst. He has trained uncountable salespeople and helped many businesses with their marketing strategies.

Today, Rich consults and speaks on management skills that help create a sales-oriented company culture.

He has a special passion for the Disney business model, and has been studying it since 1986.

Rich Hamilton is available for a limited number of speaking engagements each year.

Richard Hamilton Associates offers behavior and values profiles for staff selection and management; learning systems for sales, marketing, and advertising; and consulting services.

Contact Information:

Richard Hamilton Associates
Phone: 602.438.2345 1.800.816.7710
Internet: www.SellBetter.com
Email: info@MagicStrategy.com
Mail Care of: SellBetter, Box 50186, Phoenix, AZ 85076

The Magic Moment Recognition Package

We've put together a special package for managers who want to implement a recognition program combining elements similar to Walt Disney World's Guest Service Fanatic card program and the Applause-O-Gram program. The Magic Moment Starter Pack Includes:

- 5,000 full-color pocket-size Major Magic Moment cards.
- 150 full-color Applause-O-Gram Recognition Certificates.
- 6 copies of *Disney Magic-Business Strategy* book.
- 1 copy of *Disney Magic-Business Strategy* audio cassette program.
- The Special *Magic Moment Recognition Program Manual* to use in implementation of the program, including checklists, a special audio cassette program describing how the programs work and how to coordinate them in various sizes of companies, and information about special recognition pins and periodic celebration meetings.

How to Get Other Products

Order additional copies of this book or our other products from the web site, by mail or by phone:

www.MagicStrategy.com

SellBetter Tools, Box 50186, Phoenix, AZ 85076

Tel. 800.434.1291

Disney Magic-Business Strategy book, ISBN 097284760X, 20.00

Internet Business Magic, ISBN 0972847618, 20.00

Disney Magic Ideabook, ISBN 0972847626, 20.00

Disney Magic-Business Strategy audio cassettes, 89.00

Disney Magic-Business Strategy audio CDs, 99.00

Magic Moment Recognition Plan Starter Pack, 997.00

Products with ISBN numbers may be purchased at better bookstores. Check website or phone for current pricing and additional products.

SellBetter™

Internet Business Magic
Quick Order Form

Fax Orders: 1-800-819-9087. Send this form.
Telephone Orders: Call 1-800-434-1291 toll free. Have your credit card
ready.
Email Orders: orders@SellBetter.com
Postal Orders: SellBetter Tools, PO Box 50186, Phoenix, AZ 85076 USA.

Please send the following books, disks, or reports. I understand
that I may return any of them within 90 days for a full refund of the
purchase price for any reason, no question asked.

_____

_____

_____

Please send more FREE information on:

Other books   Speaking/Seminars   Consulting

Name:_____

Address:_____

City:_____State_____Zip_____-_____

Telephone:_____Fax:_____

Email Address:_____

Sales Tax: Please add 8.1% for products shipped to Arizona addresses.*

Shipping and Handling:
US: $4 for the first book or disk and $2 for each additional product.
International: $9 for first book or disk; $5 for each additional product
(estimate).

Payment: Check   Credit Card:
   American Express   Optima   Visa   MasterCard

Card Number_____

Name on card_____ Exp date:_____/_____
(Credit card orders must ship to credit card billing address.)
*Sales tax and prices subject to adjustment to current rates.

SellBetter™

Internet Business Magic
Quick Order Form

Fax Orders: 1-800-819-9087. Send this form.
Telephone Orders: Call 1-800-434-1291 toll free. Have your credit card ready.
Email Orders: orders@SellBetter.com
Postal Orders: SellBetter Tools, PO Box 50186, Phoenix, AZ 85076 USA.

Please send the following books, disks, or reports. I understand that I may return any of them within 90 days for a full refund of the purchase price for any reason, no question asked.

_____

_____

_____

Please send more FREE information on:

   Other books   Speaking/Seminars   Consulting

Name:_____

Address:_____

City:_____State_____Zip_____-_____

Telephone:_____Fax:_____

Email Address:_____

Sales Tax: Please add 8.1% for products shipped to Arizona addresses.*

Shipping and Handling:
US: $4 for the first book or disk and $2 for each additional product.
International: $9 for first book or disk; $5 for each additional product (estimate).

Payment: Check Credit Card:
  American Express Optima Visa MasterCard

Card Number_____

Name on card_____Exp date:_____/_____
(Credit card orders must ship to credit card billing address.)
*Sales tax and prices subject to adjustment to current rates.